My *Daddy* TOLD ME SO

WALTER L. WRIGHT

Hart Books
Fallbrook, CA 92028

Editing and page composition by Ken McFarland
Cover photography by Gary Burns
Cover and interior design by Mark Bond

ISBN: 1-878046-65-9

Contents

Dedication

I dedicate this work . . .

To my beloved wife, Jackie. Her pleading, cajoling, and downright threatening—along with love, patience, and forbearance—have resulted in this book.

To the vast Wright clan members, many of whose stories are included here.

And to the memory of my daddy, Nathan Monroe Wright, whose Christian counsel and example have helped make me who I am today.

Acknowledgments

Several people helped present this book to you,

Several people made it possible,

Several people helped us walk through:

My incomparable executive assistant, Z. Kathy Cameron, is to be commended for her inspiration and encouragement to endure and complete this work seven years after it was begun.

My good friend and "adopted" nephew, Gary Burns.

Judi Doty, for her eagle eye proofing.

Scott Moncrieff, for patience in editing the rough-draft manuscript.

Dan Houghton and Hart Research, for making publication possible.

Foreword

Little Brother,

These words need to be written. Daddy was a wonderful man, and should not be forgotten. Momma had the privilege of doing great things for God in a public way, and everywhere I go I meet people she was instrumental in bringing to Christ. Her wonderful legacy will live on. But few people outside our family had the good fortune to know Daddy. I am pleased that you are writing this tribute to his memory. The world will be richer for it. And now, here's something Daddy told me:

"A Preacher of Righteousness"

You are Walter, "Beeky," son of his mature years. Momma and Daddy had reached the age of 39. Their youngest child, Audrey, was six years old, and they assumed that they would not be adding any more children to the family. Imagine their surprise on learning that there was to be a number seven! They had feelings of apprehension and concern for this new responsibility at their ages. Thirty-nine was considered quite old in those days (1933-34).

Daddy told me, on one of my frequent trips home, that he and Momma had voiced their concerns to Dr. Alman, our family physician. Daddy said that when Dr. Alman placed you in Momma's arms after delivering you at home, he looked at these beleaguered parents and said, "Nathan, Willie, this son will be the comfort of your old age."

Daddy said the words hung in the air like a prophecy. As he watched you grow and develop, he was amazed at your ability to learn any and everything set before you. Long after all of us had left home, you remained there. No longer was Daddy's precious, limited time and attention divided among seven children. You had it all. You were able to observe him and listen to his words. You knew him better than any of the rest of us.

Every time you accomplished some new achievement, he would call me long distance to tell me about it. You were the first, and only one, of his sons to finish college. He witnessed your marriage to your lovely wife, Jackie. He witnessed the birth of your three sons, Walter, Jr., David (whom Daddy named), and Harold Jean, (named after Daddy's fourth son), and your only daughter, Lisa.

His heart thrilled when you accepted the call to the ministry "to be a preacher of righteousness." You were even his pastor for a few years. You built a lovely home right next to his. You tirelessly labored to build a new home for him and Momma. All of these things he called or wrote to me about.

His cup was full to overflowing. I wonder if he realized how much of a part he played in all of your successes? Did Dr. Alman's prophecy, "This son will be the comfort of your old age," come true? You betcha!!

— *Love, "Babe"*
(Eileen Wright Lester, big sister)

Prologue

"HIS NAME WAS DADDY"

I write this book about my father – a self-made man who found Christ as Lord and Savior. This is not a how-to book, nor is it a daily devotional. My thirty chapters are far too few to serve an entire year. It is a book of reminiscences of a relationship between a son and his father. I do not pretend to be an accomplished author, and I am sure that my flawed writing style will belie that fact.

Maybe some of the experiences shared with my dad will be a blessing to someone else. I will say this much: If your father is living, please go see him, call him, and write to him. Let him know how much you appreciate what he did for your upbringing, and that you forgive him for the mistakes he made while learning to be a parent. Make an effort to get with him when no one else is around. Talk to him and "pick his brains."

Honor him, even if he wasn't a good dad. In the process you might just gain a friend. Live out the only one of the Ten Commandments that contains a promise: "Honor thy father and thy mother that thy days may be long upon the land which the Lord thy God hath given thee" (Ex. 20:12).

His name was "Daddy." Oh, I know his legal name was Nathan Monroe Wright, and that he was born December 13, 1894, in Dayton, Ohio, but his real name was "Daddy." I used to wonder why my mother and her brothers called him "Monroe." All we kids knew he was "Daddy." When he died in April, 1981 his four grown sons and one daughter were still calling him "Daddy."

You see, he epitomized the title, the aura, the position of daddy. He provided for his seven children, brought up during the great depression. He provided for us so well that I was 12 years old before I realized that we were a poor family. We were poor in material goods, but oh, so rich in love and security and self-esteem.

Daddy was the product of a broken home. He and his two sisters, Iona and Rowena, were in a children's home for much of their young lives while both parents were very much alive and physically well. Psychological research has shown that many people reared in such circumstances are prone to perpetuate the same dysfunction if and when they have their own families. That is another reason I believe my daddy was a miracle of God.

He determined while in that children's home that if he ever had a family, he would hold it together at all costs. He made that vow come true. He, with my momma, Willie Lee Dale, created such a family environment of love, warmth, and fierce inter-dependency that each of their offspring has engendered the same spirit in their own families. However, I will be the first to admit that we children have had far less success than Momma and Daddy.

Folks used to think we were anti-social because we never visited much. Just the opposite was true. Our home was usually host to some wayfarer or friend who needed help, comfort, or just to witness love in action. Momma and Daddy stopped visiting when their brood got so large that people would invite them to social functions with the stipulation: "Don't bring your children." No, we did not go out much, and we still do not. Wrights visit each other, and there are so many of us that it keeps us quite busy. However, we have always loved people, because this is what we saw practiced by our parents. There was rarely a Sabbath meal served in our home without guests at the table. Many nights I slept on a couch in the living room because some church official or some hurting person was in my bedroom receiving the comfort I took for granted.

Daddy was bigger than life to his children. This was due largely to my Momma's teaching, because Daddy was gone much of the time making a living for us. Momma was very faithful in building his image and value to each of us. Two things we could usually count on. Daddy would be home every night, though late. I say usually because on rare occasions he would "stay on the place" at the rich estates where he worked. The other sure thing was that Daddy would be home all weekend and attend church with us.

Daddy was a very religious person with implicit trust in God. His father was a Methodist preacher and his grandfather was also a preacher in the African Methodist Episcopal Zion (A.M.E.Z.) church, having founded one in old Carnegie, Pennsylvania. It comes as no surprise, then, that Daddy founded two Seventh-day Adventist churches once he and Momma had converted from Methodism to Adventism. Those two churches still thrive today. They are the Ethan Temple SDA Church in Dayton, Ohio, and the Dale Wright Memorial SDA Church in Germantown, Ohio. In all of this, Momma was right by his side, being everything he needed. She was a tower of strength, but then, that's another book.

Daddy wasn't perfect. He was full of flaws. He talked too loudly. He never learned to whisper. He sang off key. He belched at the table without ever excusing himself. He fell asleep on company, no matter how important they were. He had one little expletive that always seemed to pop out at the wrong time. He was human, and he loved God, his spouse, his children, his country, and life itself.

Though he sang off key, no one could pitch a song for the outdoor singing band from the church like Daddy. I have never heard anyone beseech the Lord in prayer with more sincerity, sensitivity, or honesty than my daddy. He got answers too. If anyone had a need, they would rather have Daddy on the prayer line with the Lord than anyone else. God often honored this faulty, but totally honest and transparent man. He loved God with all his heart.

So Momma and his in-laws called him "Monroe." His daughters-in-law called him "Daddy Monroe." His grandchildren, great-grandchildren, and great-great-grandchildren called him "Grandpa." The church members called him "Elder Wright," but to us his name was just "Daddy."

Daddy was so full of "daddyisms" that he could have been a philosopher. In an offhanded, seemingly unintentional way he was always giving advice or counsel on some perplexity of life. I had no idea they had had such a profound influence on me until I decided to write this book. Now here it is. It is simply a book of the things my daddy told me as a child growing into manhood. These little bits of information have so gripped me in adulthood that I find it nearly impossible to preach a sermon without Daddy showing up and talking to my audience. I don't apologize for them because I know they are true. After all—

MY DADDY TOLD ME SO!

"IT'S THE BEST WE'VE GOT, IT'LL HAVE TO DO"

Oh, Daddy was as common and comfortable as an old shoe. There was no pretense, no sham, no posturing on his part. Yet Daddy was thrilled to entertain many of the leaders of our church over the years. He and Momma hosted pastors, colporteurs, evangelists, conference presidents, departmental directors, musicians, educators, and even the president of the General Conference of Seventh-day Adventists, Elder R. R. Fighur, and president of the North American Division, Elder C. E. Bradford. The most amazing thing was how readily this variety of leaders accepted that hospitality.

One conference president once said, "Sister Wright, if my travels bring me within 50 miles of your farm that will be my choice of accommodations." I know they enjoyed the good food that we children took for granted. But good food alone cannot account for the parade of distinguished guests that graced our farm.

After a sumptuous meal many of these visitors joined us in singing, playing games into the wee hours of morning, or they would lead out in extensive discussions of Bible truths. These visitors seemed to strongly connect our family to the church and its hierarchy. It also taught us respect for our leaders as we saw them in unguarded moments of plain humanity.

Now here is the surprising part. Our farm house had neither electricity nor gas, running water nor flushing toilets. No, our guests took sponge baths in basins, read by kerosene lamps, warmed by a glowing fireplace, and visited an outside toilet that we called the "privy." All the scrumptious food was prepared on a wood-burning stove, and the lemonade was cooled with ice chipped from a big block in the icebox. The butter was made in an upright dasher churn or our later "modern" hand-cranked churn. We placed calls on a 13-party line with a crank telephone.

The carpets were swept with an old Bissell push sweeper or straw broom. The dishes were washed in a galvanized tub. The soft water was caught in big barrels under the roof down-spouts. The fires were started with twisted paper, kindling wood, and wooden matches. The eggs were gathered from the henhouse, and the milk was extracted each morning and evening by the hands of this author. The crisp sheets and pillowcases the guests enjoyed were washed on a rub board and ironed with a flat-iron heated on the wood-burning range.

And still the visitors came. You would have thought we had some sort of luxury hotel hidden away in the lush green valley of Twin Creek, outside Germantown, Ohio. They loved to come because love was to be shared in abundance. No pretense, no sham, no posturing was to be found in this humble farmhouse.

The greatest miracle I ever saw Momma perform was when she made lemon chiffon pie with no lemons. The guests were enthralled. They did not know that the cupboards were bare. People always thought that we were well-to-do.

I knew we were well-to-do. With warm beans in your belly, shoes to wear to church and school, a hot iron wrapped in a towel to keep your feet warm in bed on a cold winter night, and all the love you could ever hope for, how could you be anything other than rich? "And having food and raiment, let us be therewith content" (I Tim. 6:8).

By the way, those shoes were used Boy Scout shoes that Daddy brought home from the rich folks where he worked. They squeaked when I walked in them, but what boy would be ashamed of a pair of shoes that had "Be Prepared" stamped into the indestructible soles? You couldn't wear them out, and I suppose that's why the rich kids sent them to me.

When Momma would become concerned about some special guest who was on the way to our house, I would hear Daddy say, "Mother, it's the best we've got; it'll have to do." Then they would pray, and God would use those two to perform one of His miracles.

At the age of 11 I found myself crawling around under the old farmhouse pulling wires as the electrician installed electricity. In my junior year of high school my best buddy, Bob Bevenger, and I dug the pit and trenches by hand to install the septic tank and leach lines for the flushing toilets. Momma burned the first biscuits she cooked on the new electric range, but it didn't take her long to adjust to the newfangled convenience. My sister, Audrey, got her long, flowing hair caught in the wringer of the new washing machine.

Yes, we modernized over time, but I never heard my dad complain about what others had in comparison to what he had. He never displayed a covetous spirit. He lived out the words of Hebrews 13:5: "Let your conversation be without covetousness; and be content with such things as ye have." Jesus set forth the correct philosophy. "And he said unto them, Take heed, and beware of covetousness: for a man's life consisteth not in the abundance of the things which he possesseth" (Luke 12:15). For Daddy, to have his children around him; good food on the table; heat in the fireplace; and God by his side, was all he ever needed.

Are you squandering energy trying to "keep up with the Joneses?" Relax, my Friend, and trust God. Just as with the little boy's lunch, He will take the little you have and make it a blessing to many if you just commit it to Him. "Not that I speak in respect of want: for I have learned, in whatsoever state I am, therewith to be content" (Phil. 4:11).

"Your Ma Will Be Home in the Morning, Boy"

Daddy bought a farm in 1936, but he was no farmer. The little twenty-acre farm was in the middle of Ohio's small farm country near Germantown—about 15 miles southwest of Dayton. I moved to the farm before any of the rest of my siblings or even my parents. My uncles, Harlan and Orie—Momma's brothers—had co-purchased the plot of land with Daddy. They had used a portion of their veteran's pensions from World War I, and Daddy had a servant's inheritance from one of his wealthy employers who had died.

I lived with Uncles Harlan and Orie, "Auntie Me"—Harlan's wife—and Grandpa Dale, Momma's father. I wish I had time to tell you about Grandpa George Thomas Dale. He was a Cherokee Indian, but that's another book. I learned many things living on the farm, such as milking cows.

It was my job to milk the cows before catching the school bus in the mornings and again in the evenings after school. The problem was that I also liked to play a lot. Daddy kept warning me to milk the cows on schedule. He came home early one night, and I had not done the milking. Now, if you know anything about cows, you know they soon settle into routines of regularity. It is amazing that if you milk them at a certain time for a while they will show up at the barn at that precise time, on their own, every day!

After Daddy's warning I promised to milk the cows in a timely fashion, but boys tend to forget promises that are not emphasized with incentives. Besides, Daddy had already been home early one day this week, and that was not likely to happen again for months, right? Wrong!

I was playing in Uncle Harlan's front yard as the sun slipped behind the western hills on this autumn evening. Then I heard it. The cows were bawling their heads off. That's another thing cows do. They let the entire neighborhood know it if you haven't milked them on time. I took off running up through the cornfield, heading for home. The cornfield was only stubble in late October, and there were even a few pumpkins left in the field.

I could see my breath on this cool evening as I jogged along. I could also see something else. There, silhouetted against the setting sun, was—you guessed it—my daddy! He was walking toward me with that familiar shuffling gate that could break into instantaneous speed he had developed as a racehorse exercise boy. He was swinging something in his right hand. It was three or four strands of an old corrugated rubber doormat. What were his intentions?

Now, you will understand my naiveté when you realize that at this time I was 11 years old and had never received so much as a spanking from Daddy. Please don't worry. My momma had more than made up for Daddy's lack of attention in that department. Some suggest that by the time I came along—I am the seventh of seven children—Daddy had mellowed out and was a little burned out on discipline. This was not true. As I write these words more than 60 years later, I can still feel his intensity, and I can still testify to his commitment to the great parental art of delivering stripes.

During the course of this humiliation I remember promising Daddy things I could never hope to deliver—things he didn't even want. Things so remotely connected to reality that the real wonder is how he refrained from breaking into uncontrollable fits of laughter. I made all these promises to get him to stop. But he stopped when he got good and ready. It was Daddy's strange act. It was my first and last whipping from him. Now that's what I call thorough!

My momma was away in New York City with my older siblings. They—the Wright Family Ensemble Singers— were there to sing on Arthur Godfrey's Talent Scouts Show. I remained home with Daddy. Now you know why he was coming home early every night. He didn't want his baby boy to be alone. But I was too young to figure all that out at the time.

I milked the cows, late though it was. I had supper that Daddy prepared. I went to bed still in shock that this unspeakable thing could have happened to me. Even more unspeakable was my complete misjudging of my daddy's resolve and determination to have his youngest son obey him. Then the miracle that was so typical of my daddy happened.

As I lay in bed, my body still shook uncontrollably with those deep sobs that indicate the administration of a very efficient whipping. My bedroom door swung open. Light flooded into the dark room from the hallway. Daddy came into my room. He never came into my room unless it was to wake me for summer work or to say in a softened rough voice, "Happy birthday, Beeky." That's my nickname.

Here was Daddy in my room! He walked carefully around my bed, and—with huge hands that had once molded iron at the Dayton Malleable Iron Works—he tucked in my covers, even under my chin. He looked at me shivering in the half-dark room and patted my covers.

"Your Ma will be home in the morning, Boy," he said—and he was gone!

Now I lay in my bed shivering, but for a different reason. He loved me! He cared! He had to do the whipping because I gave him no choice. I forgave him! I loved him too! "For whom the Lord loveth he correcteth; even as a father the son in whom he delighteth" (Prov. 3:12).

Sometimes our Heavenly Father must chasten us. He is patient and long-suffering toward us, but sometimes we give Him no choice. If He didn't chasten us He could never convince us that He loves us. In this regard all of us are like children. If left to our own devices we would make many bad choices and poor decisions. If allowed to do exactly as we please, without limit, we would surely assume that God doesn't care. Nothing could be further from the truth. You wonder how many times He has hovered over us with a great heart filled with pain because of some chastening we have forced Him to deliver.

If we listen carefully we may hear Him say, "Be still, my child. Joy cometh in the morning."

"For his anger endureth but a moment; in his favour is life: weeping may endure for a night, but joy cometh in the morning" (Ps. 30:5).

"YOU CAN WASH YOUR OWN BACK"

Daddy was a great example of independence and resourcefulness. I suppose much of that developed of necessity when he lived in the children's home. I can remember an incident when he was teaching me to take my own bath as a youngster. Now, you must understand that taking a bath back in 1940s Ohio farm country was no picnic.

First, you had to carry water from a well that was about 200 yards downhill from the house. This daily practice taught me to appreciate the nursery rhyme, "Jack and Jill went up the hill, to fetch a pail of water. Jack fell down and broke his crown, and Jill came tumbling after." Believe me, I fell many times fetching water from that well.

Three

Next, you had to build an outdoor fire and heat the water in a galvanized laundry tub placed over that fire. The outside of the tub always got sooty from the open blaze. Therefore, the trick was to get into the tub, take a bath, and get out of the tub without becoming dirtier than you were when the process began.

Sometimes we took baths on laundry day. That way, you could use the same water that you washed clothes in and cut the water hauling effort in half. Trouble was, if you were the seventh of seven children, the water could get a bit slippery by the time Momma got down to you.

Now back to the problem at hand. I was washing in the tub under Daddy's watchful eye, when I asked him to scrub my back as Momma always did. Daddy looked at me, raising his left eyebrow—his exclusive form of expression with kids—and said, "You can wash your own back!" Well, I never heard of such a thing! Did he think I was the India Rubber Man we saw in the circus? Did he think I could make special use of all those double joints other kids said I possessed?

He said he would teach me the method he learned in the children's home, where you had to do everything for yourself if it got done. He said, "They beat me when they taught me this, but I won't beat you." Then he took the washcloth by its opposite, diagonal corners, flipped it over his back, holding on to those corners in each hand, and began to seesaw it back and forth across his back. Magic! I could do that! And I did.

Next time Momma wanted to scrub my back, I showed her my new independence that Daddy had taught me. No problem—I could wash my own back. I've been doing it ever since, but it goes so much deeper than a back scrub. Daddy had shown me my first feeble steps toward resourcefulness. He used to repeat the old adage: "Necessity is the mother of invention." He was right.

The only dependence acceptable to Daddy was dependence on God. He taught us absolute, unwavering dependence on God. I often wonder about some of the methods God must have used to humble such a fiercely independent man. The Lord must have broken Daddy with a firm but compassionate hand, because I recall him weeping at the mere testimony of God's goodness toward him and his family. In his prayers he would thank God for "provision." I didn't know what it meant at the time, but I later learned it meant "All things come of Thee, O Lord."

"Every good and perfect gift."

Daddy not only believed that God helps those who help themselves, he also believed that God helps those who are totally helpless. He and Momma practiced it every day as they shared with others less fortunate than we were. What pride, what self assurance, what total dependence they had, to believe—as poor as they were—that some others were in worse condition.

Yes, I could wash my own back, but there were some things that only God could do for me. Daddy taught me to wait on the Lord for those things with patience and expectancy, because God never fails. "For all things come of thee, and of thine own have we given thee" (1 Chron. 29:14).

"NEVER WASTE ANY TIME AROUND A WOMAN"

Daddy never had much time to actually talk to us kids. He left most instruction to Momma, who was with us most of the time. He worked a couple of jobs just about every day to make ends meet. He had been a newsboy, racehorse groomsman, typesetter, short order cook, iron molder, butler, chef, and landscape gardener. I remember filling out job applications, and in those days, in addition to your race and national origin, they asked your father's occupation.

I would try to make up some exotic-sounding title for what Daddy did. It is difficult to make cleaning out rich folks' garages sound exotic. In those days I was sometimes ashamed of the fact that Daddy worked for rich white folks. Well, I made the mistake of hinting this to my Momma, and did she ever square me away.

Momma allowed as how I was very fortunate to have a father who worked every day, came home every night, brought her all the money, provided for my every selfish need, and practiced priesthood in our home. If I ever had any doubt as to how solid these two were, that cured me. They were a real pair, and nobody, I mean nobody, including their own children, ever came between them. If you tried, you got squashed.

Every summer and during holidays you could earn spending money by working with Daddy doing lawns or odds and ends on his many "private family" jobs. It still amazes me that these jobs were never mandatory. You would expect such a self-made man to be very demanding of his children, especially his sons. He seemed never to want us to work as hard as he did or experience the hardships he had. This guy raised seven children during the Great Depression and was never once on public welfare and never once stood in a soup line! Many of our friends and even relatives were on the public dole, but not Daddy's family. Too proud. Too resourceful. Too independent. I am still impressed.

One of those early morning trips to work gave Daddy the chance to tell me about the "birds and the bees." We paused at a stoplight. He looked over at me. "Boy, I've been meaning to have a talk with you," he said. I'll never forget it: THE TALK. I was about 14 years old. It was a little late for THE TALK, but nobody was going to cheat me out of this rite of passage. Here it comes!

He continued, "Never waste any time around a woman you wouldn't marry. You can ruin a whole lifetime for a few moments of pleasure." The light turned green. We drove off. That was it! That was it? This is all? No lectures on human plumbing? No hygienic dissertations on venereal disease? No mention of condoms, diaphragms, or teen pregnancy?

I had heard all those things at school. I expected, at the very least, that a good talk from a boy's father would have included any or all of these monumental, brain-numbing, desperately needed "facts of life." It disappointed me. I was crushed, yet relieved. Every boy wants to have THE TALK—but every boy dreads THE TALK.

Looking back, I wonder what it must have taken for Daddy to summon up the courage to talk to his baby boy on such important matters. He didn't get this from his father. He had no point of reference for doing such a thing. Upon checking with my older brothers I found that Daddy didn't do any better with them. However, this is significant: All the Wright brothers agree that Daddy was right on target. If we adhered strictly to what he shared with us we could come out just fine in dealing with the opposite sex.

Let's take another look at it. *"Never waste any time."* To Daddy, time was money. To waste time was to be less than diligent. To waste time was to squander one of the most precious things God has given. He used to say that time is talent and that everybody has that talent. I never saw Daddy waste time in my entire lifetime. He knew how and when to have fun and relax, but he never wasted time.

"Never waste any time around a woman..." To Daddy, "womenfolk" were special—a valuable gift from God. He was always polite, courteous, respectful, and tender when it came to women. He treated our mother that way, even when she, in her hot-headed Kentucky way, would get under his skin. When things really got tense between the two of them, he would leave the house and walk around the neighborhood. He always came back, they always made up, and they never let us kids in on it. It was none of our business.

"...you wouldn't marry." Well, now. It seems Daddy was recommending that we only spend time with quality womenfolk. There may be lots of women a young man might want

to hang around, but he wouldn't want to live with them for the rest of his life. Daddy was saying to eliminate them from your social calendar. Why invest time with people who will not bring good returns?

Marriage is for life. A life partner must be the very best in character, intelligence, and spiritual attractiveness you can find. Physical attractiveness always seems to take care of itself. After all, beauty is in the eye of the beholder. It is a relative and subjective aspect of choosing a partner. Daddy never gave advice on physical attractiveness. The Wrights were often accused of choosing only fair-skinned, musically inclined spouses. This, in spite of the obvious facts to the contrary. Our family, like most African-American families, includes all the beautiful hues of skin that our mixed genes can produce.

Marriage is not only for life. It is also for survival. Daddy came from a broken home. He wanted each of his children to embrace the same philosophy on marriage that he had adopted so many years before while in the children's home. Get married. Have a family. Save the children. No divorce. No separation—not even for a night. We didn't all do as well as Daddy and Momma, but we never lost sight of the principle: God hates divorce.

"You can ruin a whole lifetime for a few moments' pleasure." If I had only looked closer, there were the "facts" I so desperately longed for. When passion replaces conscience, you are headed for moral ruin. Satan is the enemy, and he has done an extraordinary job of perverting the precious, God-given gift of human sexuality. The attractiveness of sex has been so completely exaggerated as to render it as some consuming fire. God invented sex, but it was for our joy and for the procreation of the race. It was never intended to be the end-all, be-all of personal relationships.

A "few moments" of self-gratification can lead to a lifetime of regret and guilt. Daddy knew this, and he wanted his young son to avoid the pitfalls, the traps, that the enemy has set. He wanted me to hold myself in reserve for the woman I would marry—for the relationship that God could bless and that I could enjoy in the full freedom that God grants to married couples.

I have talked to my own sons and daughter about the "birds and the bees." I had more and better education to draw from than did Daddy. I had more knowledge and experience than Daddy. But I did not have more wisdom than Daddy. He was led by a "thus saith the Lord" for all his counsel. For him it was, "Trust in the Lord with all thine heart; and lean not unto thine own understanding. In all thy ways acknowledge Him, and He shall direct thy paths" (Prov. 3:5-6). You can never go wrong by trusting in God's wisdom.

My children are all grown with families of their own now. I only hope that I was able to give them something just half as memorable as what Daddy gave me on that early, chilly morning on the way to work.

"QUIET IN CHURCH"
The Raised Eyebrow

Some parents threaten their children by screaming at them. Others bring their children in line by brandishing a switch, strap, belt, or hairbrush. Daddy just raised one eyebrow. He could simply look at you, raise one eyebrow, and with one withering stare, reduce you to ashes. He didn't have to say a word.

One Sabbath morning the church service seemed exceptionally long and boring. Our visiting pastor, whom we saw only once every few weeks, was there. He was always long and tedious in his delivery. He would speak a phrase and pause for what seemed to be interminable moments, then move on to the next phrase. Even the adults were driven to distraction by this plodding style of delivery.

On this particular Sabbath it may have been the pastor's slow pace—or it may have been the continuous repetitions of standing and sitting that the congregation was doing. You stand for prayer. You sit. You stand to sing. You sit. You stand to welcome visitors. You sit. I, along with my little church buddies, usually kept pretty good track of all these exercises, and thus would know at any particular time in the service approximately how many more stands and sits we had to do before we stood for the benediction.

I don't know how I lost count, but I did. Usually, after the benediction our church was quite noisy. People would immediately begin to greet each other and participate in loud, animated conversation as they exited the building. We hadn't invented the long, tedious dismissal by pews that most church ushers use today.

We stood for prayer. Somehow, I miscounted. I thought it was the benediction. I expected loud talking and laughter. I let out a war whoop to express my relief for rescue from such a boring service. It was the expression of freedom coming from a little four-year-old boy who had been on his best behavior for what had seemed to be half a day.

To my utter dismay, the congregation was again seated. Every eye of the 200 or so congregants was fixed on me! I was seated next to my older brother, Paul, and his new wife, Bessie. They were glaring at me in disbelief and total embarrassment. Even my little buddies were staring at me in wide-eyed amazement. I had just done something each of them would have loved to possess the nerve to do. It did not matter to them that my outburst had come as a result of total miscalculation and error. The deed was done, and I was a hero.

Trying to slide beneath the pew in mortified horror, I glanced toward the rostrum, where my Daddy, as head elder, always sat. Yes, he was scowling at me, and . . . the one eyebrow was raised! It was lifted in an unbelievable arch higher than I had ever seen it before. I stopped in mid-slide, frozen by his look and absolutely terrorized by its implications.

How does a little boy sit for the remainder of the service after such humiliation? I began to softly cry. That's right. If you are four years old, you can always cry. Thank the God of heaven for mothers. Mine came and rescued me, taking me out of church for what I assumed would be the mother of all switchings. Yes, Momma usually used a switch, because she didn't have an overactive eyebrow as Daddy did. But this time, instead of punishment, she comforted me and assured me that my daddy was not going to kill me after service. He and Momma must have discussed it, but he never mentioned it to me to the day he died.

What gave him such control with just a lifted eyebrow? It wasn't that he had beaten me unmercifully on some prior occasion. I only received one whipping from my Daddy, and that wasn't until I was 11 years old. It wasn't that I had witnessed punishment to my brothers and sisters. When I came along in the family, Momma and Daddy had long since stopped using physical punishment on my siblings. My sister, Audrey, was six years older than me, and I had never even seen her get a switching. What was it? How did he do it with just a look?

Well, the look carried a promise. It was the promise of the execution of ultimate justice and authority. It was down-to-earth, unquestioned, non-negotiable authority, but it was mixed with mercy. He was never unfair, never unjust, but always in charge. My daddy was my first look at God.

In addition, I believe it was a thing called honor. Or, as the Scriptures put it, "Honour." Exodus 20:12 says, "Honour thy father and thy mother: that thy days may be long upon the land which the Lord thy God giveth thee." We honored Daddy because he was due honor. He had earned our respect and honor from our first days of consciousness and cognition. We didn't think he was God, but he was the way we wanted God to be.

Parents should never forget that they are the first impression their children get of God. The type of authority practiced by parents will suggest the type of authority practiced by our Heavenly Father. Children are very impressionable and in their early development are unable to distinguish one authority figure from another. If the child experiences harshness and lack of mercy from the parent it transfers to his or her picture of God. We can't be too careful in setting the right example of firmness mixed with love, of chastening mixed with compassion, of showing our displeasure with wrongdoing mixed with mercy. God is like that. And so was my daddy.

"You Should Only Eat Green Apples Fried"

It was a fact when I was a child. We liked to eat green apples. You know, right off the tree, long before they had an opportunity to mature into the lush golds and reds that indicate ripe fruit for eating. The culprits were my nieces and nephews and me. Let's see—there was "Punj," "BC," "Tommy," "Sis," "Punka," and "Sherry." Only four years and ten months separated me from Punj, and there was only five years between me and BC.

They were more like my little brothers and sisters than nieces and nephews. Of course, I didn't tolerate any such notions in them. It would have meant loss of stature and quite a degree of leverage had I slipped from "Uncle Beeky" to just plain old Beeky. That uncle thing assured me of dominance right into adulthood. It should come as no surprise that I was the ring leader in most of the mischief that aggravated my daddy so much. But oh, how handy it was to have a few other names to toss into the hat when retribution was due.

Daddy hated for us to raid the apple trees for green apples. He told us all of the old stories that adults always told kids to keep them away from unripened fruit. "You'll get a stomach ache." "You'll get terrible cramps." Well, I've got to tell you, I don't remember ever having any bad effects from eating green apples.

We loved to pick them, take them out to the cow pasture, and rub them on the big salt blocks Daddy kept for the cows. You know—cows lick more salt, they drink more water, they give more milk. Well, that old block of salt looked so inviting in the smooth, white indentations left by the cows' slurping tongues. We couldn't help but rub our green apples on it and enjoy a farm kid's delight!

No, we never got a disease or any ill effects from that either. Maybe farm kids have special stomachs, or maybe God is especially merciful to farm kids. It is probably more of the latter, because now I am sickened just at the thought of licking where a cow has just licked.

Daddy said, "You should only eat green apples fried." We kids knew that was certainly one option, but it wasn't the only one. On the farm we ate several things that were green and fried. There were green tomatoes, dipped in egg batter and rolled in cornmeal, then fried to a golden brown. There was eggplant prepared the same way. These things kept us alive and well nourished when things were really tough down on the farm. They weren't considered delicacies by the kids. They were necessities. But you don't eat necessities when you are a kid and you want to have fun and live a little dangerously at the same time. So what would you eat? You ate raw, green apples—that's what.

No matter how much Daddy threatened, cajoled, or menaced, we could not be stopped. Each spring season we could be found high in the branches of the old apple trees, gathering fun for the day. Daddy loved us all, and we discovered that his bark was worse than his bite. What we probably needed was a painful outbreak of the stomach ache. Or maybe a painful outbreak in another part of the anatomy.

One day Daddy came home unexpectedly and caught us in the trees. He had the biggest stick you have ever seen, and we thought it was Judgment Day for sure. How strange to see him brandishing that big stick! It was totally unlike him. He growled and groused and shouted a lot, but he never waved the weapon. We all escaped the swing of that stick, but green apples never held quite the same appeal after that strange episode. Maybe he really would "go through you like a dose of salts," whatever that means. We were cured.

Aren't many Christians that way? God warns of so many dangers, but we love to live dangerously. We think we know best. We know the penalties, but when nothing happens to us, we begin to think nothing ever will. We become calloused in sin. We start to take God for granted. We believe He loves us too much ever to harm us.

Well, He does love us—even more than Daddy loved his grandchildren and his youngest son. But one day, the Bible tells us in Isaiah 28:21, God will rise up in anger and shall "do His strange work . . . and His strange act." When He does, I want to be on the right side, converted and surrendered to Him. Our Heavenly Father desires that, long before that time, sin will lose its appeal for us, and we will be totally His.

"KNOCK HIS BLOCK OFF"
The Unfortunate Bull Calf

I have already said that Daddy was not a farmer, but he loved farming. Part of it was his sense of duty to family and church. He believed that he should rear us away from the corrupting influences of the city. He also believed that it was his religious duty and that we could all be better Christians on the farm. Daddy's grandfather, Ralph Ford, was a very good farmer who had run a farm near Springboro, Ohio, when Daddy was a boy, and Daddy's fondest memories as a child had to do with that farm.

Many times he would tell us of rising early; eating a hearty breakfast; drinking fresh, cold milk; and working hard enough to be famished at the noon meal. Then they ate a light supper before retiring, and it started all over again the next day. Daddy wanted to recapture those days for his kids. It didn't happen exactly that way, but we were blessed to be living on the farm as we grew up into adulthood.

Since Daddy wasn't much of a farmer, he did things on the farm in a very unconventional way. I learned much about farming from attending Germantown, Ohio, Elementary School and High School, where I graduated. The children with whom I attended school were, by and large, farmers. I picked it up from them. Daddy knew and respected this, but sometimes he expected too much of me.

We had cows, chickens, and turkeys, and my oldest brother, Dale, experimented with a few ducks. We raised corn, wheat, a vegetable garden—and my brother, Harold, experimented with sugar cane for making sorghum molasses. It was a farm, but I am sure we were the laughingstock of all the German-bred farmers on the surrounding farms.

Did I mention that Daddy was unconventional in his approach to farming? One day we were to round up a bull calf that had been fattening for the market. Daddy didn't have a truck or trailer as did the other farmers, so he was attempting to load the calf into the back seat of the family car. You heard me right!

Each time we rounded up the calf, heading him for the open rear car door, it would bolt away to the left or right and go careening down through the pasture, tail sticking straight up into the air, bucking and kicking, to be chased and coerced until the same scene was repeated. Daddy was getting fed up. He yelled and screamed and chased until Momma was afraid he would have a heart attack.

On the next roundup, Daddy had us all stand to each side of the open car door, forming an aisle for the calf to approach. Daddy said, "This time, if he bolts, I'll knock his block off." Well, we didn't see anything in Daddy's hands, so we felt it was just another figure of speech, for which Daddy was well known. The calf approached cautiously, weaving from side to side, rolling its eyes, looking for the opening that would again grant him freedom.

At the last possible moment the calf leaped to the right! It was the wrong way to leap. Daddy was over on the right side. In an instant he had balled up his fist and hit the calf a mighty blow right between the eyes! The calf shivered, dropped on all fours, and was out cold! Daddy picked up the calf—weighing all of 400 pounds—and threw it into the rear of the car, where he had removed the back seat cushion.

We all stood there spellbound. Not only were we impressed with the awesome strength shown by our father, we also had a new respect for this man we called "Daddy." The older boys thought it would not be at all wise to challenge this man. We always thought he was Superman. Now we had the evidence.

Have you ever experienced the relentless aggravation of temptation? Like a bull calf, just when you think you have it corralled, it jumps out of control once again. We know this is Satan in all his frustrating best, trying to discourage us until we yield and give him the victory. I believe the apostle James has a solution that Daddy could agree with.

In James 4:7 we read, "Submit yourselves therefore to God. Resist the devil, and he will flee from you." The submission is surrender to God rather than to your temptations. This process provides omnipotent power to be an overcomer. This overcoming is resistance. More than human strength can then be summoned to resist, the next time the enemy comes around. In so many words, James seems to be saying: "Knock his block off." That's right! By the power of Almighty God, you can lay a lick right between his eyes and just "knock his block off!"

"IF HIS FACE IS WHITE, HE'S DIRTY"

Daddy worked as a hired domestic for most of my life. That is, he was a chef, butler, and landscape gardener for various rich white folk in a very exclusive area of Dayton, Ohio, called Oakwood. As such, he had an intimate view of his employers. He cooked meals, served big social parties, and manicured the lawns of some of the most influential people in Montgomery County.

He also learned to take a lot of guff from the more cruel and insensitive of these employers. It is amazing to me that Daddy was not an out-and-out bigot and that he did not teach racism to his children. On the contrary, he and Momma were very adamant about fair play and giving each person you meet the benefit of the doubt. And they developed this philosophy during the 20s, 30s, and 40s in a very racist

America. We were not allowed to speak disparagingly of any race or nationality.

We were very much aware of the struggle for equality for Colored people, because we met it every day. You consciously thought first about entering a store or other business establishment operated by white owners in those days. There was the ever-present fear of rejection. Will I be served and treated with respect—or will I be turned away and publicly humiliated? It was so much a part of growing up in America that it followed me into adulthood.

I can remember writing to a campground in Colorado in the early 1960s to determine if I and my little family would be welcomed or rejected. I wanted to protect my wife and three little boys from embarrassment or something worse. The owners of Chief Hosa Camp in Golden wrote back a beautifully assuring invitation to "come on out." We vacationed there for the next three years.

In 1976 when Jackie and I went house hunting in Bridgeville, Pennsylvania, we had lots of fear and trepidation. I remember sitting in the waiting room to interview for a condominium. Jackie nervously turned to me and said, "Walter, they are not going to accept Black people in here." And then we noticed some promotional pictures on the wall. Bless your soul, there was a Black man and his wife having a barbecue in their back yard. I said, "Well, they've got at least two here—why not us?" We bought the house and lived there for four years until reassigned to Columbus, Ohio.

The point is, we were still intimidated by the racism of our childhood, way down in 1976. Where did we get our self-esteem in the midst of such a dehumanizing system? We got it from very durable, proud parents.

Every so often, my daddy would come home from serving a party or some other social function in disgust. His shoul-

ders would sag, his chin would be set, and his face—normally wreathed in smiles—would contort. Then out would come
those bitter words tinged with the disappointment of another
broken trust, another delayed dream.

"If his face is white, he's dirty," he would say. Momma
would comfort him, and we kids would give them room and
privacy. We were not allowed to hear those discussions between a hurting father and the noble woman who stood by
his side. They did not want us corrupted by their temporary
disillusionment.

Since I was the "baby" of the family, I could sometimes
wander into these private moments that Momma and Daddy
shared. I would hear her remind him that not all white folks
were deceptive and treacherous. This puzzled me, because
Momma was usually the one who complained to Daddy
about some unreasonable demand that had been made on
him or some humiliation to which he had been subjected.

During those times Daddy would defend the "folks," and
he could always end the discussion with, "Willie, I've got to
make a living, and this is the only thing they will hire a Colored man to do who only has an 11th-grade education."

Yes, every so often, Daddy's cup would boil over, but the
general trend of his life was fairness, optimism, and true grit.
In the bad times he and Momma seemed to be the perfect
match for each other. When either of them got off the track
of what they believed and espoused, the other would gently
nudge that spouse back to high ground, where they could
please God and be a good example to their children.

How did Daddy bounce back from the brink of bigotry
and racism under such conditions? Well, Momma helped
him, but they both had something going that would be well
for all to copy. They believed in the Golden Rule. More than
that, they believed in the Holy Scriptures.

"But I say unto you, Love your enemies, bless them that curse you, do good to them that hate you, and pray for them which despitefully use you, and persecute you" (Matt. 5:44). The words of Jesus are so comforting when we face injustice and unkindness. Daddy learned, long before he died, that if your face is white it does not necessarily mean that you are dirty. It simply means that, like all the rest of us, you are imperfect and in desperate need of a Savior.

The 45th verse in Matthew 5 continues: "That ye may be the children of your Father which is in heaven: for he maketh his sun to rise on the evil and on the good, and sendeth rain on the just and on the unjust." That's one thing Daddy really wanted. His fervent desire was to be a child of the King. I thank God that Daddy taught us children correctly, even before he was able to live up to it himself.

"TELL ME ALL ABOUT IT"
Vicarious Victories

Daddy was a high school drop-out. He left school in the eleventh grade. He had held the dream of being an attorney, and he would have been a good one. He would have been an even better history teacher. He loved history. In fact, he loved learning. His mind was like a big sponge, soaking up information from a wide variety of sources. Here was a man who could converse knowledgeably on so many topics, yet with very poor grammar.

He called food recipes "receipts," and invariably called rent receipts "recipes." He only rarely pronounced people's surnames correctly, yet he could enthrall you while talking about

Charlemagne and Napoleon. He would make you think you were witnessing the Roman Church's pope being taken captive by Napoleon in 1798. With "Tippecanoe and Tyler, Too," the Battle of Bull Run, the Battle of the Bulge, or the assassination of President William McKinley, Daddy could keep you spellbound! I have never heard any theologian describe with more feeling or clarity the history of the ancient Hebrew sanctuary and its services, or our relationship to a living, soon-returning Savior.

But he felt limited, unprepared, and disadvantaged. He decided to enjoy success vicariously through the accomplishments of his children. He was so very proud of each of us. He kept a big scrapbook on a table next to his favorite chair. It contained yellowing news clippings and pictures of every major event involving his progeny. Thank God we were able to fill his book many times over.

When we individually or collectively returned home from some event, he would lean out to the edge of his chair with a twinkle in his eyes and say, "Now, tell me all about it." He didn't want any cursory report, either. "Blow by blow and click for click" is the way Daddy wanted it, with every detail in place. Can you imagine the positive self-esteem and feelings of importance this imparted to the children? We knew we were important to him. We had his undivided attention, and interruptions were unwelcome and rebuffed. Sometimes, he would say in disgust, "Well, just save it until I can hear the whole story. There is too much confusion going on in here right now."

This was his practice when Audrey got a good mark in arithmetic, Eileen got her first teaching appointment, Dale once again received first prize in fine art at the Montgomery County Fair, Bill was appointed to a position with the Army Map Service during World War II, Paul produced Daddy's first grandchild, Harold became owner of the first Black-operated AM/FM radio station in Ohio, or when one by one all four of my offspring were born on Sabbath. He duly took note, and vicariously experienced and enjoyed it all.

He never missed a single radio broadcast or video telecast of our family for the 26 years we were in the public media. We actually made requests on the air for Momma and Daddy to have certain food prepared for us when we arrived home from the radio station. They faithfully complied each time. He loved this notoriety. He was a very proud man.

This started a tradition in our family. Until Daddy died, each Friday evening my brothers and I came to his home to review the week. We had long since moved from under his roof, but he still wanted to hear all about us—our hopes, dreams, defeats, and victories. And we still wanted to share them with him. Many times he helped us with solutions. Other times he led us to discover insights that solved our problems. Either way, the real comfort came from knowing that he cared and that he would listen attentively without interruption. I believe that's how it is with a good father.

Our Heavenly Father is keenly interested in all our goings and comings. He cares about our plans, hopes, defeats, victories, and challenges. He always listens without interruption to every word we place before Him. "Come now, let us reason together, saith the Lord: though your sins be as scarlet, they shall be as white as snow; though they be red like crimson, they shall be as wool" (Isa. 1:18).

Sometimes He gives us answers so clearly that we think we hear Him speaking. Other times He leads us in circuitous routes to discover solutions we could never learn any other way. Either way, it is so comforting to know He cares. Every moment of our lives He leans forward over the battlements of heaven with a twinkle in His all-seeing eyes and says, "Now, tell me all about it."

❀ ❀ ❀ ❀ ❀ ❀ ❀ ❀ ❀ ❀ ❀ ❀ *Ten* ❀ ❀ ❀ ❀ ❀ ❀ ❀ ❀ ❀ ❀ ❀ ❀

"WE ALWAYS OPEN GIFTS ON CHRISTMAS EVE"

Thanksgiving, Christmas and New Year's were always high points of celebration at the Wright household. We looked forward to these times because Daddy, more than any other person, made the observance very special. I am certain it resulted from another of the resolutions he made during a rather deprived childhood.

He determined that if he ever had a family there would be adequate recognition of high holidays in his house. He made good on this self-promise. He was a different person during the holidays. It seems you just couldn't aggravate him enough for him to lose his temper during these times. Daddy believed these fun times were for kids, and he even schemed to make the time special.

There was no guarantee of gifts at Christmas, but there was a guarantee. There would be mountains of fruit, nuts, and hardtack candy, and the celebration would start Christmas Eve. There would also be dinner in abundance, a tradition that has grown and expanded over the years in our family.

When new members joined our family in the persons of daughters-in-law or sons-in-law, they were accustomed to opening gifts on Christmas morning. I guess the whole world does it that way, but not the Wrights. When they questioned, Daddy would say, "We always open gifts on Christmas Eve."

My uncles, Momma's brothers, actually started the tradition because they could never endure the suspense of waiting for the normal Christmas morning opening. Neither the Dale family, Momma's maiden name, nor the Wrights were taught to believe in Santa Claus so why wait? We all knew that Daddy brought whatever gifts there were so let's get on with it.

I was a grown man before I knew the added dimension to Daddy's fixation with Christmas Eve. When he was a child, his father showed up unexpectedly one Christmas Eve and took him and his sisters from the children's home to have Christmas at home. I guess that *would* give special significance to the day.

It was quite a scene. Daddy always cut the tree himself from out in the woods. Sometimes they were the most forlorn, scraggly trees imaginable, leaning precariously to the left or right. We all laughed and poked fun at Daddy's trees. He bore it well and could not be deterred from making his annual pilgrimage into the woods to bring back his tree with boyish delight.

All the gifts would be placed under and around the tree. When we grew older and had jobs we all contributed to the mountain of gifts that were on display. Some late shoppers, my sister Audrey being the perennial worst offender, even rushed in with their gifts still in store bags, and names hastily scribbled on the outside.

Daddy would step forward, take his place on a stool next to the great pile, and have a brief devotion of thanksgiving to God, the real Provider. Then, we all held our breath as he called the first name. Cheers went up after each name, and we excitedly tore into our packages. We were sometimes knee-deep in wrapping paper as this ritual came to an end. More than once someone's gift was scooped up with the paper and tossed into the roaring fire that Daddy always had burning in the fireplace for these occasions.

It never mattered how much you received, but only that your name was called. It would be a disaster if Daddy didn't call your name. That would mean you had been overlooked or forgotten. In all my years I never saw any of us left out.

Sometimes it was a truck with a wheel missing, or some other well used toy that Daddy had rescued from the trash bin at one of the rich homes where he worked. The toys always looked beautiful to me. And my name was called. There were times when my gift was a brown sack with a popcorn ball, nuts, an orange, an apple, taffy and hardtack candy. It was wonderful. And my name was called. One year it was a small Bible inscribed with a message from Momma to me. I cherished it. And my name was called.

When returning to public school after Christmas vacation ended, the children all gathered to ask each other what they had gotten for Christmas. It was only then that I was ashamed of some of my gifts. They didn't seem to compare to the long lists that many of my schoolmates recited. Sometimes I made up things from my imagination or "wish list." How could I explain to them the total delight of hearing Daddy call your name out in front of everybody? They would never understand that the main thing was to be included.

I once heard a man say, "I would rather be a door keeper in God's kingdom than a prince in the devil's kingdom." I was too young then to understand the full import of what he said, but now I do. One day Jesus will come for His children. Some will be expecting Him later, but He will come early because He is anxious to save us. What an awesome time! It will be the thrill of a lifetime to hear Him call your name out in front of all the universe.

The order will not matter. Just call my name. The place assigned in the kingdom will not be important. Just call my name. Some important people will be missing, but please, call my name. It will be a tragedy beyond comprehension to be left out. Jesus said, "Rejoice not, that the spirits are subject unto you; but rather rejoice, because your names are written in heaven" (Luke 10:20).

We always opened our gifts on Christmas Eve because we couldn't wait another minute for the special joy of sharing. Soon Jesus will come because He can't wait another minute to share the joy of His kingdom. Don't miss it. Be there! Listen for your name!

❀ ❀ ❀ ❀ ❀ ❀ ❀ ❀ ❀ ❀ *Eleven* ❀ ❀ ❀ ❀ ❀ ❀ ❀ ❀ ❀ ❀

"HAPPY BIRTHDAY, BOY"

Daddy had seven children—five sons and two daughters. He knew and remembered each child's birthday without fail. He didn't plan parties, he didn't bring gifts, and he didn't send cards. Momma did that part. But Daddy always came into your room very early on the morning of your birthday and gently awakened you. He would announce, "Happy birthday, Boy!" Then he would be out of the room and on his way to work before you could recover. You wanted to say, "Thank you, Daddy," but he was gone.

How did he remember each one? He not only remembered each birthday, but he enjoyed recounting the circumstances of each child's birth. We were all born at home except Bill. Daddy recalled the weather, the time of day, and the location. We

50

moved often, so that latter item was extraordinary. How did he do it? I believe it was because he really cared about us—each one of us. To Daddy, each child was unique and special.

Daddy didn't play favorites, but sometimes we suspected that his oldest daughter, Eileen, was his favorite. Later, when we were all adults, we would tease him about Eileen. He would protest that Eileen was the only child that had moved away from home, and therefore he missed her the most. She went away to college, and upon graduation she moved away to New Jersey to take her first teaching assignment. We all missed her.

In his declining years Daddy never made the mistake of having to call the roll of all his children before he came to the name he wanted. Momma did this often when she grew older, but Daddy never did. He knew each child in his or her uniqueness, and he kept us separate in his mind.

Daddy loved the very concept of family, and the more of us that were around at any given time, the more satisfied he would be. He was never happier than when he was drifting off to sleep with a roaring fire on the hearth, and his children were over at the piano singing the sweet, complex harmonies that were the trademark of the Wright Family Ensemble Singers. But in his thinking, we were never homogenized into one single lump. We were each precious to our daddy, and he never let us be in doubt about that.

After reaching adulthood, each of my brothers and I would visit Daddy and Momma in their home every Friday night. Whichever son arrived first was welcomed with open arms and much anticipation of what the evening's discussion would bring. One by one we arrived, until all were present. It was enjoyable, quality time spent with a father who was very busy in his younger life but who was now very happy for time spent with his "boys." If one of us didn't show up, he was disappointed.

If Harold, Paul, and Walter were present, he would still ask, "Where is Bill?" (Dale was already deceased when this tradition was started.) He would do the same for whichever one was missing. We each had value to him, and one couldn't replace the other. He wanted each of us. He cared about each of us. He knew each of us.

Yes, he knew us, because he cared about us. He took the time—and I still don't know where he found it—to be acquainted with each of us. Daddy was proud of the fact that Dale, William, and Paul were excellent artists and that they made a living that way. He was so happy that Eileen was the first of us to get a college degree and work as a teacher in the schools of the Seventh-day Adventist Church.

Daddy gloried in Harold's entrepreneurial abilities, and I often heard him speak of Harold's industriousness. Of all of us, Harold was most like Daddy in this respect. Harold was always able to get a job, and he would find you one too, if you didn't mind working.

Audrey made Daddy proud as she became a graphic artist and master printer. Toward the end of her life she enrolled in chaplaincy training for hospital service. Daddy would relate this to anyone who would listen. Of course, I became an ordained minister in the church that Daddy loved. I know the personal satisfaction that he got from hearing me preach.

Early on, when I wasn't very good at it, he still encouraged me. After my sermon he would pass by me at the church door and say, "Walt, that sermon showed lots of study." Yes, he encouraged me, but he wouldn't lie. He cared, but he wouldn't pretend.

Are you aware that our Heavenly Father knows each of us intimately? Oh, He knows us so very, very much better than Daddy ever could have known his children. The Lord watches with extreme interest as we make our way through this life. But more than that, He interferes in our lives when we allow it. When we welcome it, God is happy to influence our ways. It is a mystery why more people don't invite Him into their lives.

What was Daddy really saying to me as he appeared to me early in the morning of my birthday? He was saying, "I love you." This was difficult for Daddy to put into words. He said it often to Momma, but he didn't verbalize it to the children.

The Lord has no such problem. In Jeremiah 31:3 it is said of Him, "The Lord hath appeared of old unto me, saying, 'Yea, I have loved thee with an everlasting love: therefore with loving-kindness have I drawn thee.'"

It is not exactly "Happy birthday, Boy!" But the same caring, knowing attitude of a loving father that knows each of his children individually is much in evidence in this passage. It kind of makes you want to say "Thank you, Father."

"BONE OF MY BONES, FLESH OF MY FLESH"

I don't know how Daddy learned to be so affectionate. With Momma and his girls, that is. I believe he thought he had to be gruff with us boys, and so he was—except on birthdays and holidays. He came from a dysfunctional home where not much affection was shown, but somehow, he was a hugger and patter from way back.

He really couldn't pass Momma in the house without touching her. Oh, it was all moral and kosher in front of us kids, but he was truly Momma's lover. He would take her in his arms sometimes and lift her completely off the floor. He would squeeze her until sometimes she squeaked. He petted her with his big, heavy hands and she would protest, "Monroe, you'll jar my insides out!" Then he would roar with approving laughter and say, "You're bone of my bones, and flesh of my flesh!"

Momma always protested, but not too much. It was like some game they were playing. Daddy pursued Momma, and she pretended not to like it. It was great fun, and we kids really enjoyed it. We knew that Daddy loved Momma, and she loved him back. There was such a feeling of security and well-being in our house that it is no wonder that we developed into affectionate, balanced adults.

There were times when Daddy and Momma would do the dishes together. This was after I came along. I understand that when my oldest three brothers were young it was their chore to do the dishes. I never saw that, so I have to take their word for it. What I did see was Momma and Daddy at the sink doing dishes. They would sing together—usually some Negro spiritual. Momma was a great singer; Daddy was just a singer.

I can remember, "Swing low, sweet chariot," and Daddy would steal a kiss between phrases. Me and my sister Audrey would hide behind the door and giggle during this ritual. We felt warm and loved because our parents were so obviously in love.

Late in life Momma became a Bible instructor, and she would go away each summer for up to 12 weeks to assist some evangelist in tent crusades. We all missed her, but Daddy missed her most. Every Friday night at an agreed-upon time Daddy would phone her wherever she was in the country.

Daddy accepted no foolishness at these times. We had to be absolutely quiet so that he wouldn't miss a word Momma said. It was always late at night after the meeting had closed. Daddy wanted the schedule of topics the evangelist would deliver. He particularly wanted to know when the "Law" and the "Sabbath" would be presented and how the audience reacted to these cardinal messages. He prayed daily for Momma that God would protect her as she went door to door in some of the roughest neighborhoods in America.

Momma worked with the foremost Seventh-day Adventist evangelists in America. There was Wilmot Fordham, George Rainey, John Wagner, Jr., J. Malcolm Phipps, Henry M. Wright, R. Leslie Willis, and C. D. Brooks, to name a few. She also honored me by working as my head Bible instructor in two of my tent campaigns.

She never related the really dangerous situations until after she returned home. That was wise, because I believe Daddy would have called her home if she had been too specific. Daddy wouldn't spend a phone call for any other reason than to call Momma when she was away. Sometimes it was agreed that she would call him. He would sit by the phone near the appointed time, warning all in the house to be quiet.

Momma's homecomings were great. She used to travel to her appointments by train, and later, by airplane. We all saw her off and welcomed her home, no matter what the mode of her transportation. I can remember crying at the sight of her plane disappearing into the sky down at the Boone County Airport outside Cincinnati. It was almost too much for me to bear, knowing I wouldn't see her for 10 to 12 long weeks.

We all—and I mean the entire family: in-laws, grandchildren, everybody—would wait in the train depot or airport to greet Momma when she returned. My brothers would paint huge "Welcome Home, Mom" banners, and other people in the terminal would think some famous VIP was coming in. They were right. It was our mother, and Daddy was there, more excited than any of us.

Every Mother's Day my daddy would spade up a big circle in the front yard and plant Momma's favorite flowers. There were petunias, snapdragons, violets, and marigolds. Daddy would arrange them all in colorful patterns. Then, leaning on his shovel, he would call out, "Willie, come and see." Oh, how he would beam with pride as she came out of the house oohing and aahing with delight.

Daddy bought Momma a pair of I. Miller shoes for every birthday. They were extremely expensive in those days, but he never failed. I can only imagine how long he had to scrimp and save for those shoes. They were accompanied by the mushiest birthday card he could find. We always demanded that she read these aloud to the whole family. She would stammer through them, blushing and smiling, as Daddy stood there, head down, with the biggest grin you could imagine. At those times he looked like a big kid himself.

What was going on between these two? It was a lifelong commitment to love that grew in intensity with each passing year. It was a love hammered out on the anvil of time, which included hardship as well as good times. Did they ever disagree? Yes, but we children seldom got to see it. Their personal lives became more and more private as they grew older.

Daddy and Momma believed in Malachi 2:14-16. The Lord hates divorce and warns against dealing treacherously with the wife of your youth. He wants us, as married couples, to be one in Him. In an age when people are afraid to make a commitment, it is good for me to remember the deep commitment of my parents.

When a marriage works, it is a miracle from God. Two people come together from different backgrounds and attempt to form a union of cooperative bliss. Even within the same culture there are tremendous challenges. Yet God commands us to become one with our spouses. How can it be done? We need the sacrificial spirit exemplified in the phrase, "Bone of my bones, flesh of my flesh."

Adam looked at his new bride in Eden and knew she was part of his very being (Gen. 2:22, 23). He must have looked upon her with awesome pride and tenderness. They entered into this incredible equation: 1+1+1=1. It doesn't work in arithmetic, but it works in God's reckoning. 1 Man + 1 Woman + God = 1. That is the only way we can be one. Without God we come up with all types of erroneous solutions. If you get any number but "1," that is an indication that God is not part of the equation.

Fall on your knees and ask Him. He is anxious to make you one in Him. If both parties are willing, the Lord can work a miracle of restoration, even if the marriage has been sadly spoiled by indiscretion, unfaithfulness, or insensitivity. Try God. Hold on to Him tenaciously. You just might hear the throaty roar of a pleased and loving husband ring out in your house saying **"You are now bone of my bones, and flesh of my flesh."**

Thirteen

"BIG BOYS DO CRY"

Have you ever heard anyone say "Big boys don't cry"? A little boy falls down, skins his knee, starts crying, and out comes this lame attempt at reverse psychology. "Now, now, big boys don't cry!" What a shame! I consider this to be one more instance where society is shaping a boy into a future unfeeling, uncaring, insensitive man.

I have seen men on television in a situation that obviously calls for honest grief and even tears. They will pretend that something is in their eyes that must be wiped away. After all, if big boys don't cry, then certainly grown men can't cry. All grown men remember the admonition that big boys don't cry.

We weren't taught that in the Wright household. If the situation called for tears, you were allowed to cry, no matter how old or what gender. In fact, if Momma laid a switch of correction to that part of the anatomy God prepared to receive it, you had better cry. The sooner the better! And it was really funny—or rather, it's funny now. It wasn't funny at all back then. If you put too much into the crying, according to Momma's evaluation, she would say, "Now dry up, or I'll give you something to really cry about."

My daddy was the most all-out man I have ever known, but he knew how to cry when the time was right. He didn't apologize, and he didn't pretend to do something else. He cried openly when extremely happy or extremely sad. I and all my brothers cry without shame, because the man we most admired in life also cried.

I wouldn't doubt that this is one reason women outlive men, on average. They can cry, and it is expected of them. Think of the emotional relief that crying provides. You turn it loose, you let it go, and you feel better, as you begin emotional healing.

I saw Daddy cry uncontrollably twice in my life. The first was in May of 1953 when my oldest brother, Dale, was killed in an auto accident. Dale was the choir director of the Ethan Temple Adventist Church in Dayton. It was called the Second SDA Church when Daddy founded it. Dale was driving home to Germantown late on Saturday night after directing the music for a wedding rehearsal. I passed him on the highway, and he blew his horn in recognition. I blinked the lights on my little 1938 Ford, because my horn didn't work. I never saw my big brother alive again.

Two miles and three minutes later, he slammed into a concrete culvert on Manning Road and was killed instantly. My brothers Paul and Harold, with their wives Bessie and Eleanor, found Dale and his wife Rudy on the side of the road, still in their car. Fortunately Rudy was only badly injured— but Dale was gone.

I heard a long, horribly grief-filled wail come out of the back bedroom where Momma and Daddy had been asleep. I stumbled into the room, wiping my sleepy eyes, and was given the news by Bessie. Daddy cried. Oh, how he cried. He was inconsolable for a while. Then he began to remember the precious promises of our Lord.

The second time I heard Daddy cry without comfort was in February 1979. He had received the word that Audrey, his second daughter, had been killed in an auto accident just one mile from where Dale had died on Manning Road. Daddy cried with a broken heart. Two of his children had preceded him in death, and he couldn't believe it. Then again, he remembered the precious promises of God.

"But I would not have you to be ignorant, brethren, concerning them which are asleep, that ye sorrow not, even as others which have no hope. For if we believe that Jesus died and rose again, even so them also which sleep in Jesus will God bring with him" (1 Thess. 4:13, 14). These words are a blessing to those who believe, and Daddy believed.

Does God cry? Well, we know from Luke 19:41 and John 11:35 that Jesus wept. There certainly isn't any doubt about Jesus being all man. Nor should there be any doubt about Him being all God. When we insist on a disobedient course of life, we bring grief to the heart of God. We can only imagine what God must have felt when his son, Adam, and his daughter, Eve, rebelled. He knew immediately they would one day have to die. It was because of His own immutable law that they would die.

And then the second Adam, Jesus Christ, God in the flesh, died to pay the awful price for all sinners. Don't you believe the Father cried? His commitment to our salvation was unwavering as He viewed the scenes of Calvary. Every time we perform a rebellious act, we bring back the sorrow. We must surrender all and stop this needless sorrow. We must face the fact that sin is sorrow, and that big boys, little boys, and even grown men need to cry until we sense the real seriousness of our actions. Then we can turn back to God and stop the crying, not because we are too manly, but because the great Comforter has wiped away our tears.

❀ ❀ ❀ ❀ ❀ ❀ ❀ ❀ ❀ ❀ *Fourteen* ❀ ❀ ❀ ❀ ❀ ❀ ❀ ❀ ❀

"DON'T TALK WITH YOUR MOUTH FULL"

Supper time in our home was the best of times. Each child had a reserved seat, and we sat in that seat for every meal. Daddy sat at the head, and Momma sat at the foot of the table, when she sat. Momma rarely sat down for the Sabbath meal. She stood near the sideboard watching us and making sure we were well served. Sometimes, she would sit down and eat a small meal when we were all finished. Not even Daddy could talk her out of this.

The food was exceptional. Even weekday food was good, though it lacked the variety of a Sabbath meal. There would be a huge pot of green beans with whole or half Irish potatoes floating in the beans. Sometimes it would be a pot of cabbage with potatoes. And other times there would be dandelion greens garnished with boiled eggs cut in half and placed around a gigantic platter. The best of all was great northern soup beans with potatoes floating and cornbread standing tall.

Do you get the idea that Wrights eat lots of potatoes? Well, you're right. We eat potatoes like other people eat rice. Rice was a cereal to us, eaten with milk and sugar. I know that makes real rice eaters sick, but that's the way it was.

After every meal the pot was clean and polished. We wasted nothing. We even drank the juice off the dandelions. Momma called it "pot liquor," and it was the best natural laxative you could want. Left-over cornbread was crumbled up in buttermilk the next day for a special treat. No, there wasn't much variety during the week, but I never remember going to bed hungry.

Sabbath meals were an extraordinary experience. When Daddy was head elder of the church in Dayton, we took a huge kettle of chili for Sabbath lunch. Many members of the church would lurk around until Momma invited them to lunch with us. One lady in the church once said, "The Wrights' boiled water even tastes good!" Well, we never served boiled water, but you get the point.

On those special occasions when we had Sabbath meals at home it was a real celebration. The variety and quantity was abundant. Momma was not a dietitian, but she had a theory for feeding nourishing food to her family. Momma said that if you have a variety of colors on the plate, it will be a balanced meal. I can't find any fault with that plan even today. We also had dessert on Sabbath, which could range from peach cobbler to Momma's specialty—lemon chiffon pie.

Sunday mornings were special too because it was the only day of the week when we ate breakfast. Fried green apples in season with hot biscuits, scrambled eggs, and of course, fried potatoes. It didn't matter what day or what meal. Each meal was a happening, because it was family time.

There was a happy atmosphere at our table. We talked animatedly, and it seems that all the world's problems were solved there. At least all the problems pertinent to children living in the care of loving parents were solved. There aren't that many problems, you know. There were times when I would get so excited I would blurt out something unintelligible with a mouth full of food. It always elicited the same response from Daddy. "Boy, don't talk with your mouth full."

I noticed that older people didn't have to swallow all their food before speaking, and it was a decided hindrance to good communication for me, too. But that was the rule. Maybe it was because I sprayed several people around me with food when I got excited. Maybe it was because I often got choked talking with a mouthful. Maybe it was because of something older folks called "good manners." That was the rule.

Old folks used to say, "Children are to be seen but not heard." The supper table was the exception. The children were welcome to participate in the family discussions—if your mouth was not full. Daddy didn't talk much at the table. He sort of ate and listened. Then when we needed a decision, a judgment, or a summation, Daddy would render it. That was it. Discuss all you want until Daddy gave the final word, then no more discussion. I did notice a few times when Momma would have the last word, but those were usually the times when Daddy asked what she thought about a given situation.

You didn't argue with Daddy, and you didn't address him with your mouth full. You respected his wisdom, position, and preferences. Oh, what unmitigated gall we humans must have to argue with God. We ask His opinion, and if we don't like it, we whine and complain and argue.

It's a little bit like talking with your mouth full. We are so full of ourselves and our own opinions that we blurt out directions to God on how things should go. If we really knew the answers we wouldn't have to consult Him in the first place. And in the second place, if we really respect Him as Lord and Savior and the preferences He has for our lives, we should swallow hard and accept His will. When we approach the Lord, we should be ready for the summary. Scripture tells us, "Let us hear the conclusion of the whole matter: Fear God, and keep his commandments: for this is the whole duty of man" (Eccl. 12:13).

The next time you want to address the King of the universe—who also just happens to be our Savior and Friend—first swallow self, pride, arrogance, and ego. Then speak clearly, deliberately, and with confidence, knowing that the One who hears all and is concerned with every detail of our lives will look up, summarize the situation, and give you an answer you can count on. Talk to Him as long as you want. Just don't talk with your mouth full.

"DON'T LET ANYBODY DRIVE YOUR CAR"

The year was 1952, and I was a Junior in high school. One of Daddy's very rich employers had given him a 1938 Ford two-door sedan. It was that anonymous gray color so common in the 1930s. The little car was immaculate, without spot or wrinkle. It had been stored in a garage for most of its life, and the tires were dry rotted. Everything else worked quite well.

The radio, with its tiny dial and speaker, was a joy. The squeaky little horn made you think of Henry Ford every time you heard it. The cloth upholstery was in mint condition, and the windows had a slight amber tint. This was a classic car—a real treasure! The most shocking part of all is that Daddy gave it to me!

There were not many rules. Curfew of 11:00 p.m. did not change just because I was now the proud owner of an antique car. I had to purchase my own gasoline. I must always let either Momma or Daddy know where I was going to be. And finally, "Don't let anybody drive your car."

Well, that last directive was totally unnecessary. I wasn't about to let anyone drive my car. My close friends either couldn't drive—or they didn't have driver's licenses. No, I wasn't about to let anybody drive my car. No, Siree, Bob!

I was driving home one afternoon with my girlfriend, Dottie. It was a beautiful Sabbath afternoon. I had a lead part in the Spring Operetta at Germantown High School, and the performance was to open that night. Dottie said, "Please let me drive!" I broke out into a cold sweat. "Do you know how to drive?" I asked. "No, but I want you to teach me," she replied.

I would like to say that I'm not sure how it happened. In this day and time no one seems to take responsibility for their own actions. We always look for another person to blame, but I know exactly how this happened. I was too weak to say "No" to a young lady that I was still in the process of trying to impress. She was a lovely person—not at all evil—and there is really nothing wrong with a guy teaching his girlfriend to drive his car, unless he has made a promise to his father as a condition of ownership.

We were less than a mile from my home. That point is significant because it says that my Daddy was likely to see her driving my car in direct disobedience to his instructions. I was willing to incur the wrath and displeasure of my Daddy, the giver of this wonderful gift, just so that I could please my girlfriend. It is amazing how bold and brash we can be in disobedience.

I was already in the process of "leaving father and mother to cleave unto my own wife." No, we were not married, but I at 17, and she at 14, were certain that we were going to be married. It hurt us so much when adults would suggest to us that we were only experiencing a "crush" or "puppy love" that would fade away. Well, it did, and each of us married some other person when true love came along. But I am ahead of my story.

I parked the car on the side of the road and exchanged seats with Dottie. It was a special joy to put one arm around her as I gently gave instructions on the clutch, the brake, the gearshift knob, and the accelerator. It was a special joy, but I'm sure it didn't do much for her efficiency or focus in learning to drive.

She pressed the clutch, eased the shift into first gear, raced the engine a little more than was necessary or safe, quickly released the clutch, and we lurched off down the road. She really did pretty well until we rounded the bend near my house. She made the bend, but on the wrong side of the road! By the time I grabbed the steering wheel to right us, we were off the left side of the road and into the ever-waiting tree. Crunch!

I banged my head on the rear-view mirror, drawing blood. If I had not been sitting so close to the driver, I probably would have escaped injury, as she did.

My head was bleeding, my heart was pounding, the left front fender of my pride and joy was horribly crumpled, and I had to walk the rest of the way home to get Daddy to come and pull me out of the ditch.

I told Daddy that I had run off the road. He allowed as how I had been driving since I was 15, had driven trips of hundreds of miles taking him and Momma to camp meeting, and that it was very unlike me to have such a silly mishap. It was a long time before I told Daddy the truth about what really happened that day. Of course, he already knew and was just waiting for me to confess so that he could tell me that he had forgiven me. He went on to explain that his disappointment included not only my disobedience but also my lie, which indicated I did not trust him enough to tell him the truth.

Do you see how illogical sin is? I thought I had lied to Daddy to keep from hurting and disappointing him. I had only compounded his hurt and disappointment. Satan is tricky. He makes a perfectly illogical thing seem absolutely plausible if we listen to him. Dottie had done nothing wrong. She had made no promise to her father about the car. She had made a reasonable request, and I had made a totally unreasonable and irresponsible reply.

Isn't it astounding that once you start lying, you must continue to cover the previous lie? Jesus said, "Ye are of your father the devil, and the lusts of your father ye will do. He was a murderer from the beginning, and abode not in the truth, because there is no truth in him. When he speaketh a lie, he speaketh of his own: for he is a liar, and the father of it" (John 8:44).

Here is one instance when we can choose our father. When we confess our sins, we choose God as our father. We reject the devil and all his sleight of hand. And when we confess, we discover that God already knows of our infractions and has just been waiting for us to come to Him so that He can show us He has forgiven us. He is disappointed when we disobey Him, but He is hurt very deeply when we attempt to cover up rather than come to Him for the forgiveness, cleansing, and healing that He longs to give.

When we refuse to come to Him, we are saying that He can't be trusted to be just and fair and kind and good to us. Satan will repeat his oldest of lies to you: "God is unjust and a tyrant." We really know better, but it sounds so logical. Trust in God, follow Him, and obey the rules. There aren't many, and they are not grievous. And by the way, when He puts you in charge, don't let anybody else drive your car.

"I CAN COOK IT, BUT I CAN'T PRONOUNCE IT"

Daddy was a professional chef. He cooked in some of the finest private family kitchens in Oakwood, the exclusive, old-money section of Dayton, Ohio. He would prepare for and serve parties of 125 guests and have them raving when they left for home. Sometimes the guests tried to lure Daddy away from his current employer. Getting and holding good domestic help was a cutthroat business in those days.

When the parties or dinners were large, he would hire his wife and children to assist him in preparing and serving. Momma was his salad chef. She made the most beautiful salads and canapés you would ever want to see. My sisters and sisters-in-law often assisted in the common, menial preparations such as peeling potatoes and onions. Each of these ladies turned out to be an excellent cook in her own right.

Daddy's crepes and blueberry muffins would melt in your mouth. His eggnog was the talk of the town. Did I tell you that once a year, on New Year's Eve, Daddy and Momma prepared these same fixings for us kids? That's how I know how good this exclusive food was. But Daddy couldn't pronounce many of the highbrow French names for the dishes he cooked with such artistry. As mentioned before, he called them "receipts," and he called proofs of purchase "recipes." When Momma would try to correct him, he would say, "Well, I can cook it, but I can't pronounce it!"

It is still amazing to think of a chef displaying such amazing attention to detail, yet he never considered it of sufficient importance to learn the proper pronunciation of these exquisite culinary delights. Amazing, yes, but it really shouldn't be surprising. Daddy always knew what was really important.

Having a well-tilled garden to raise food for the family was important. Having a well-groomed lawn to impress our neighbors was not. Having a huge family room for all his clan to gather was important. Having an attached two-car garage for the car was not. Having all his family in church each Sabbath was important. Having his family in high society was not. Having us all prepare for heaven was important. Receiving world acclaim for our musical gifts was not. The ability to cook some of the most exotic dishes known was important. Being able to pronounce their names was not.

Daddy's theology was pretty much the same. I have heard him explain the difference between justification, sanctification, and glorification. But he didn't really care. What was important to him was the fact that Jesus died on the cross to make possible salvation to all who believe and accept His sacrificial gift. Daddy knew for sure that the blood of Jesus is sufficient to save and that without it there is no salvation.

I remember one occasion when Daddy and Momma were bringing a series of Bible studies to a close. They had been holding cottage meetings in this certain home for a number of weeks, and now it was decision time. They were a beautiful Bible instruction team. They made things so clear that you couldn't be confused. It was so clear that a little four-year-old son, playing with a truck in the corner, began to grasp the truth of the very complex subject of the cleansing of the sanctuary. I learned, when they thought I was only playing.

Well, the host lady began to protest and make excuses as to why she didn't believe she was obligated to make a decision about serving Jesus Christ. After a while Daddy stopped, looked her squarely in the eyes, and said, "Madam, God will be God if you never decide to obey Him." That lady never made a decision for eternal life, and she was one of the very few who ever studied with Daddy who did not become part of the Seventh-day Adventist Church.

So you see, he could be very particular about important things. He believed with all his heart in Joshua 24:15, where it says, "And if it seem evil unto you to serve the Lord, choose you this day whom ye will serve; whether the gods which your fathers served that [were] on the other side of the flood, or the gods of the Amorites, in whose land ye dwell: but as for me and my house, we will serve the Lord."

That is clear, unambiguous, and right down Daddy's alley. You don't need all the technical jargon. Just follow the Lord. No heavy theology, just simple faith. That was my daddy's faith. He would probably say, "I may not be able to explain it all, but I believe it all." That should be good enough, Daddy. That should be good enough.

"SAVE IT FOR A RAINY DAY"

Daddy never lost his touch for wooing Momma. It felt good to all of us. Following this good example, we gave gifts to Daddy and Momma for birthdays, Christmas, and their anniversary. Momma used her gifts and kept them much in evidence. Daddy, on the other hand, put his gifts away. He actually hoarded them. We would agitate him to wear or use our gifts. He would respond, "Don't worry, I'm saving it for a rainy day."

It had to be a reflection of his early life of abject poverty. He seemed always to have a fear of running out of things. It wasn't that he was especially materialistic. After all, how materialistic can you be with seven children to rear? No, I think he had a terror of ever returning to those days of being without the necessities of life.

Daddy did the family grocery shopping. He saved coupons, scoured the newspapers, and drove from store to store to secure the very best bargains for his meager earnings. He bought shortening in 25-pound vats, flour in 50-pound sacks, and the ever-cherished white potatoes in 100-pound sacks. We gathered eggs from our chickens, milk from our cows, and most vegetables from our garden. But Daddy could never raise enough potatoes to satisfy the potato craving he had trained into our family.

I can remember rationing during World War II. Many items were rationed, and you had to have ration stamps to purchase things like gasoline, automobile tires, shoes, and nylon hosiery. But shortening, sugar, and other foodstuffs were also rationed. Daddy and his married sons would pool their stamps to make the large-quantity purchases necessary to feed our big family. We churned sour cream to make our own butter, and it was good!

Daddy was accustomed to hardship. He tried his best to shield us from it, and he did a pretty fair job of it. As I stated earlier, I did not realize we were poor until I was about 12 years old. I am sure my older siblings were quite a bit more aware of it than I was. Somehow, on my 15th birthday there was a brand-new J.C. Higgins Flyer—an actual balloon-tired bicycle! Then, when I joined my high school orchestra, there appeared a brand-new alto saxophone from Sears & Roebuck Co.

How did they do it? At the time I had no concept of the sacrifices they must have made to make those purchases possible. I actually had a tuxedo for my junior, then senior proms. How did they do it? They did without the personal things that would have made life easier for them. It didn't matter. Daddy was going to live out his aborted childhood through me, his youngest son.

I am happy to announce that the "rainy day" finally arrived for Daddy. No, I don't mean that things got worse or that Daddy became so destitute that he was forced to dig into his stash of sweaters, socks, gloves, underwear, pajamas, or Romeo slippers. No, what really happened was that Daddy learned to depend upon God, totally. That must have been very difficult for a self-made man.

In his last years Daddy worked in his garden because he wanted to, not because he had to. He wore the gifts and enjoyed them. He still shopped for groceries, but now it was a hobby with him, not a necessity.

The last 30 years of Daddy's life were much different from the first 56 years. He learned that he was only the instrument that God used to provide for the family. He was not the end-all, be-all of our existence. God was the Provider, and Daddy was the conduit. He learned this, but it does not change the fact that he was more than willing to be used of God. He gladly filled his position. He was the strongest man I have ever known.

There were finally no more "rainy days" for Daddy to dread. He spent his last thirty years hoarding the precious promises of God. Promises such as: "...and, lo, I am with you always, even to the end of the world" (Matt. 28:20). "And they shall be mine, saith the Lord of hosts, in that day when I make up my jewels; and I will spare them, as a man spareth his own son that serveth him" (Mal. 3:17). "...for I will contend with him that contendeth with thee, and I will save thy children" (Isa. 49:25). "For the Lord Himself shall descend from heaven with a shout, with the voice of the archangel, and with the trump of God: and the dead in Christ shall rise first" (1 Thess. 4:16).

This is mighty good stuff. My recommendation is similar to Daddy's: "Save it for a rainy day."

❊ ❊ ❊ ❊ ❊ ❊ ❊ ❊ ❊ ❊ *Eighteen* ❊ ❊ ❊ ❊ ❊ ❊ ❊ ❊ ❊ ❊

"BITE YOUR TONGUE"

It was 1942. We drove my sister Eileen and my brother Harold to Dayton to catch a train to Huntsville, Alabama. They were going away to Oakwood College for the first time. We were all a bit nervous about this adventure. We had lived in Ohio all our lives, and now two of us were heading for the Southland. Daddy was very concerned for his offspring.

He gave them explicit instructions on how to act. Now, Daddy had never been south in his life, but he knew certain things from reading and listening to the radio. First of all, you had to get up and move to the back of the last car on the train when you got below the Mason-Dixon Line. Colored folks talked a lot about the Mason-Dixon Line in those days. History tells us that it was the surveyor's line that formed the border between the northern and southern states.

We believed that things were decidedly different above and below this line. We had yet to learn that the main difference was that racial bigotry and "Jim Crow" were under the surface in the North—and out in the open in the South. But it existed strongly in both areas.

At any rate, they had to shift to the back of the train upon leaving Cincinnati. Momma had packed them a lunch, because Colored folks could not eat in the dining car, either. Then there was the problem of my brother being a cocky kid raised in Ohio. Daddy knew that they might encounter some racist to whom Harold might respond with something less than the acceptable respect for that time. So Daddy's instruction for such an encounter was: "Bite your tongue. If you bite your tongue, you can't say something stupid."

Many years later, Eileen told us of Harold's antics on the train. She said that every time a white person came near them, Harold would turn toward her and chew on his tongue in mock derision. He always had a great sense of humor. But he did not have a sense of the danger that Daddy knew.

Daddy bit his tongue quite a lot as he worked for the rich and privileged. Many times they spoke in his presence about "lazy, no-good Coloreds." They spoke as if he were not even there. It is a tough thing to be considered less than human and invisible. Daddy's blood would heat up, and then he would remember the wife and children counting on him. He would bite his tongue and work on.

Momma would never have taken such abuse from anyone. She was very outspoken on racial matters. One day we were in a service station, and the attendant referred to Daddy as "George." When Daddy responded without comment, Momma went ballistic. She chewed into Daddy, reminding him that his name was not "George." Then she turned on the attendant. It was not until the man gave Momma a smart comment that Daddy took him on. He was accustomed to biting his tongue, but that did not include abuse of any of his family members—and certainly not his beloved wife.

My daddy was no "Uncle Tom." He was all man, but he did what he had to do to get by and take care of his family. Once, in junior high school, a male teacher slapped me so hard in the face that it cut my lip. Momma related the incident to Daddy and my older brothers. When she saw my brothers heading out the door for the high school basketball game being played that night, she called on Daddy to stop them. She was terrified to see that Daddy was backing the car out to accompany the boys to the game. Only the grace of God prevented my brothers and Daddy from finding the teacher that night.

How do you learn to bite your tongue or turn the other cheek in the face of injustice? I believe that this same grace of God can make it possible. We are so quick to defend ourselves or to justify ourselves.

Have you ever thought back over an incident and think of all the things you could have said that would have made you the unquestioned victor? Pride and pride alone prompts such an unprofitable waste of time. Our pride doesn't want anyone to think they have gotten the best of us. That was just what Daddy feared for Harold on his first trip south.

The only way to conquer the prideful spirit is to surrender that spirit to Jesus Christ. He then stands in our stead in the encounters of life. Instead of speaking out in self-defense, we will speak with the calming, comforting words of the risen Saviour. "And my tongue shall speak of thy righteousness and of thy praise all the day long" (Ps. 35:28). If you can't do that, just bite your tongue.

"I ALWAYS WONDERED IF YOU UNDERSTOOD"

We were all gathered in the Wrights' family church just outside Germantown, Ohio, one Sabbath afternoon. It was time for YPMV—Young People's Missionary Volunteer Society. That's what we called it in the Adventist Church back in those days. It later became just MVS, and later still was changed to AYS, Adventist Youth Society, which is less cumbersome but fails to obviously indicate the mission of the organization. But I digress. Let me get back to what my daddy told me.

My siblings and I were presenting a program at YPMV, which gave us a chance to reminisce and rehearse what it was like to grow up in the Wright household. We spoke of our material poverty and our emotional and spiritual riches. We talked about our clannishness and our need to entertain those outside the family circle. Of course we recalled the most delicious food ever eaten by mortals, which our parents set before us regularly, and the sometimes horrendous food we encountered on our many singing tours. Eventually, the program brought us around to discussing our parents and the blessing it was to mature under their tutelage.

We described Daddy's hard work and sacrifice, when he really would rather have been home surrounded by his large brood of children. Our Momma constantly explained his long hours and sometimes harsh demeanor—and built him up to hero status in our eyes. We recalled seeing him cut out pasteboard pieces to cover the holes in his shoes at night, rather than buy a new pair. This sharing went on for quite a while, as each one of us remembered something special in our personal experience with our parents.

Then suddenly, it happened. Daddy, sitting on the back pew with Momma, where he sat since retiring from active ministry, began to cry. Yes, this crusty, hard-shell man, this role model of stoic manhood, this tough-as-nails leader of men, began to cry. He blurted out, "I always wondered if you understood!"

It was difficult to continue the program after that. Each of us wanted to rush back to Daddy and reassure him that we always knew of his sacrifices. Children may often be demanding and selfish, but they are not idiots. They are aware of their support and the source of their wellbeing. They just often neglect to show gratitude.

Well, when the program concluded, Daddy was showered with hugs and kisses and handshakes, to make sure that he knew we understood. Have you taken the opportunity to express to your parents or guardians the appreciation they are due? Have you thanked them for the sacrifices they made of things and activities so that you might enjoy some desire of your heart? Have you been gracious enough to thank them for requiring you to be in the house at what, at the time, seemed to be a totally unreasonable hour? Have you gotten around to admitting they were right when they protected you from the little pointy-headed boy who had only one thing on his mind—or from the little girl who had learned too early what she could do with her body?

If you haven't, get to it! I am so glad that we were able to express some of these things to Daddy and Momma while they could appreciate them, but I can't help but think we were a bit tardy. Why should Daddy have gone through so much of his life wondering if we understood? Shouldn't we have been showing him all along?

If earthly parents and guardians appreciate hearing of our gratitude, what about our Heavenly Father? I hate to think that God looks at me and says, "I wonder if he understands that sometimes I must chastise him, or deny him some desire, or delay an answer that he is demanding today." I am convinced that if we could see the whole picture as the Lord sees it, we would change nothing that He guides us through. He is all-wise and loves us with an unconditional love that qualifies Him to do for and to us exactly as He wishes. In our selfishness, we sometimes get in His way.

Let us take the time to thank our Heavenly Father, as well as our earthly fathers for our upbringing. David has a perfect AYS program to present to your daddy. It is Psalm 103. Let me quote just the first five verses here, but you read it all. It will make you grateful.

"Bless the Lord, O my soul: and all that is within me, bless his holy name. Bless the Lord, O my soul, and forget not all his benefits: who forgiveth all thine iniquities; who healeth all thy diseases; who redeemeth thy life from destruction; who crowneth thee with lovingkindness and tender mercies; who satisfieth thy mouth with good things; so that thy youth is renewed like the eagle's" (Ps. 103:1-5).

Oh, thank You, Heavenly Father, for all your wise and loving ways! Please keep us in the hollow of thine own hand until Jesus comes to claim us from this earth.

"Men Like Flowers, Too"

I sometimes wondered why Daddy took so much time with flowers. Oh, for sure, he made a living as a landscape gardener, but there was more to it than that. He really loved seeing things grow. What he lacked in farming knowledge, he more than made up with what he knew about his vegetables and flowers.

He would spade the soil and transplant beautiful flowers that were far more elegant than the remainder of the yard around our farmhouse. It seemed that his favorites were marigolds and peonies.

These plants really had to grow and flourish for him, because he offered a prayer before planting flowers and vegetables. He fully expected God to bless his plantings, because, after all, they were God's creation. We all ate from Daddy's garden, and we all decorated from his flower beds.

One day, in response to my questionings, he explained that the beauty of nature knows no gender preference. Though societal norms would have only women receive flowers as gifts, he knew that men could enjoy the delicate, aromatic plants as well. He marked me for life. I like nothing better than to see some plant, flower, or tree grow and mature with my care and God's blessing.

I learned early that you don't plant and then desert what you've planted. You must continue the watering, weeding, aerating, and feeding. You must guard against insects and drought, heat and wind. You dare not give up simply because a plant shows some stress or weakness. It is the plant needing the most that gets the most attention.

Oh, how much like God is the faithful gardener! He watches over us with tender, loving care. When we give our lives to Him in trust, he doesn't leave us to fare for ourselves. When we show signs of stress from the everyday trials of life, He comes to refresh us with some special experience. When we flag and fall over from the weight of sin, or stumble in temptation, He applies the insecticide of His love and the eradicating power of Jesus' blood.

In response to this special care, we stumble to our feet and trudge on in faith. After a while, we gain strength to carry on and even flourish. We begin to bear fruit and give off the sweet aroma of a life fully surrendered. Like many flowers and other plants, we drop our seeds, and new saints take root near us. Then the whole process begins again.

If Daddy loved to see things grow, how much more must our Heavenly Father love to see us grow in His grace and by His tender care? "The wilderness and the solitary place shall be glad for them; and the desert shall rejoice, and blossom as the rose" (Isa. 35:1, KJV).

Twenty-one

"DON'T BLAME GOD FOR YOUR TROUBLES"

I am not sure if it is human nature, but it certainly seems common to Americans. I mean the tendency to blame someone else for our mistakes and shortcomings. We are not prone to say, "I made a mistake," or, "I really used poor judgment." Even the court system is sympathetic to the plea, "My mother abused me, so I am now an abuser," or, "My hard upbringing is responsible for my mean spirit." Some will say, "My father deserted me when I was a child; therefore, I have no sense of paternal loyalty."

Well, as stated in an earlier chapter, my daddy had a most difficult upbringing—an absent father and a mother described in legal papers as "dissident." But he decided his life would be different, his family would not be dysfunctional, and he would find and share the love he had not received.

A man like Daddy is not going to be very sympathetic to someone's whining and crying about their lot in life. He would support and encourage if you were down, but he would not join in any pity parties.

I was attempting to raise the down payment for a house in my newly assigned pastoral district. The money was not available. It was one of those "I feel so sorry for myself" moods when I came to Daddy. I made the classic mistake of saying, "I wonder where God is while I'm suffering? Why would He give me all this trouble?"

Straight as an arrow, the response came back: "Boy, don't blame God for your troubles! All the good things that have happened to you came from God. You have made some bad choices and decisions, and none of them are God's fault! You need to fall on your knees and beg God for forgiveness, and then get up and start over. Then you will see that God never left you, even while you were falsely accusing Him!"

Whew! My first thought was, "Why did I ever go to Daddy?" My next thought was, "What a blessing to have a father who will steer you right and not succumb to whining and complaining!" After he finished "reprimanding" me he climbed into his car and drove out of sight.

He left me there to ponder my own stupidity in blaming God, but he wasn't completely finished with me. He reappeared in about thirty minutes with an envelope he shoved at me. I realized when I opened it that he had gone to his bank and withdrawn money to help me with the down payment on a new house. What a father! What a daddy!

I have a Father above who is even more helpful. He hears me grousing and murmuring, and yet He is always there. Even when I blame Him, He "reprimands" me and supplies my needs. "Do not fear, little flock, for it is your Father's good pleasure to give you the kingdom" (Luke 12:32, NKJV).

Twenty-two

"YOU MUST BE EDUCATED, EVEN TO DIG DITCHES"

Daddy often expressed sorrow in not reaching his educational goals, and he dreamed of his children going farther than he did. He fully realized the value of a good education, and he also appreciated the extra value in Christian education. He and Momma encouraged and enrolled the four youngest of their children in church school. There is a special dimension in learning, when you are being taught by godly teachers.

Somewhere along the way, Daddy decided to live out his dream in me, his youngest child. It must have been very frustrating for him as I wavered between becoming a pharmacist, a scientist, a teacher, or a physician. And these all came after my childhood desires to be a fireman or pilot. Never once did I aspire to being a minister of the gospel. He and Momma just continued encouraging and praying. Believe me, prayer changes things.

His admonition was always the same: "Stay in school and get a good education. In this day and time you've got to be educated even to dig ditches." He kept pushing me as I grew up in a farm community, where the average farmer had a fifth- or sixth-grade education. He didn't want me to get sidetracked or to become satisfied with less than I was capable of achieving.

Daddy was terribly disappointed when I dropped out of college after one year. I worked at all types of jobs, most of them very menial. He was very pleased when I accepted the call to ministry, but Daddy died before I returned to college, so he never saw his dream completed. He will be surprised when again we meet.

He was right. A classmate of mine was accused by our high school principal of only being capable of being a ditch-digger. He and I laugh when we meet today. He finished his education, as I did. He is now a successful excavator and ready-mix concrete producer. He does dig ditches (more correctly, those who work for him dig the ditches) but his education was invaluable to his success.

Daddy never dreamed that I would become a church administrator, but he was ecstatic when I accepted the call to enter the ministry. He would be so very pleased to know that I have served in the higher levels of the Church he loved. There is no way it could have happened if I had not vigorously pursued Christian education. He paid for the first part—I paid for the latter. One day, on streets of gold, I will tell him just how far his dream and God's leading took me in this life.

If we prepare, God will use us. If we surrender, God will guide us. If we listen, God will teach us. "All your children shall be taught by the Lord, and great shall be the peace of your children" (Isa. 54:13, NKJV).

❀ ❀ ❀ ❀ ❀ ❀ ❀ ❀ ❀ *Twenty-three* ❀ ❀ ❀ ❀ ❀ ❀ ❀ ❀ ❀

"WHEN VISITING A LADY FRIEND, KEEP YOUR HAT IN YOUR HAND"

Daddy had great respect for women. I think this is a miracle, since his own mother deserted him and set no good example of womanhood for him. Momma said that he was very popular with the girls at Steel High School in Dayton, where they attended. In adulthood he had many lady friends. In fact, he had such a reputation as a ladies' man that I understand Momma's parents were not too keen on his calling upon her for dates and courting.

This being the case, Grandma Liza Dale always assigned Momma's sister, my aunt Evie, to accompany these young people on their outings. Daddy used to howl with laughter as he related to us how he used to buy Evie a pint of her favorite chocolate ice cream as a bribe to get rid of her for an hour or so. Then he could walk hand in hand with Momma down by the levee of the Great Miami River—a favorite courting spot for the youth and young adults of their day.

This contact with a shy, retiring young woman did much to teach him respect for women. He saw the closeness and caring exhibited in the everyday lives of the Dale family. He noticed Momma's brothers and the sensitivity and deference they showed to their sisters and mother. He watched Grandpa George and the tenderness he displayed with his wife and daughters. Daddy picked it up. He recognized that this is how it was supposed to be, rather than the brawling and disrespect he had witnessed in his upbringing.

He was an unlikely candidate to marry Willa Lee Dale—youngest and most favored daughter of the Dale clan. He smoked cigarettes, his language was coarse, he was a high school dropout, and he was not trained in the ways of a gentleman. But oh, was he a quick learner! And he had good points. He was a hard worker, always employed; he may have been the best-dressed young man on Dayton's west side; and he displayed a gentle and courteous nature that belied his rough past.

Well, he won over the Dales. More correctly, he won Momma's parents—the brothers were still not convinced that this guy they saw in the streets was a fit suitor for their baby sister. But the approval of Momma's parents is all that was needed. He married his beautiful bride on October 15, 1915. He became the Sunday school superintendent of the Methodist church where all of Momma's family held membership.

A few years later, Daddy and Momma led her entire family into the Seventh-day Adventist Church. In fact, they founded the first African-American Adventist church in Dayton, Ohio. Along with them came my two oldest brothers, Dale and William. Daddy stopped smoking instantly by a miracle of God. He became the head elder of this new congregation.

What kind of advice could this father give to his young son on the social niceties of courting the ladies? In an earlier chapter I shared with you his first attempt at talking to me about "the birds and the bees." As I matured, there would be more to follow that first scary attempt.

One day, he just said it. "When you visit a lady, keep your hat in your hand." What? I was old enough to respond that way now. I wanted more, and he gave me more. He explained that Satan has all kinds of entrapments for young people and that you should never fully relax while dating. The "hat-in-hand" metaphor, in Daddy's mind, meant to stay on the alert. It meant to watch carefully, so that no enticement could lead you into activity unsuitable for a Christian couple.

Was there a biblical principle involved? Oh, yes, there always was with Daddy. Once he was fully converted, he always sought for a "thus saith the Lord." And here it is: "Watch and pray, that ye enter not into temptation: the spirit indeed is willing, but the flesh is weak" (Matt. 26:41). These precious words of our Lord were a guide for my daddy, and they seem fit and appropriate today for people of all ages.

Twenty-four

"STREETCARS AND BUSES: THEY ALL COST A NICKEL"

At first blush, Daddy might have been considered tight, even stingy, but nothing could be farther from the truth. I have talked about his hoarding tendencies, his coupon clipping, and how he grew a garden to save money. He was cautious and a bit wary because of the poverty he had known. But was he stingy? Oh, no!

My siblings said that Daddy would walk the many miles from the family home in Audubon Park to his places of employment in Oakwood. These were both suburbs of Dayton. He made this trek in all kinds of weather, since he didn't own an automobile. They described how he would arrive home late in the evening, feet wet from the snow or rain, and the cardboard-in-the-shoes ritual would be repeated.

I had to ask Daddy about this activity to see if it was really true. He explained that it was, indeed, his practice and that there was a very practical reason for it all. I was told that money was so scarce that he dare not spend it on a pair of new shoes when he had a family of six (before I was born) to feed, clothe, and shelter through the Great Depression.

He explained in addition that he carried a nickel in his pocket so that, in the event there was an emergency at home, he could take a streetcar or bus to get home quickly. He said, "Streetcars and buses all cost a nickel in those days." I was struck dumb! What kind of man is this that I call "Daddy"?

Stingy? Tight? Oh, don't you dare think that about him! His was the very spirit of sacrifice. There was absolutely nothing too good for his wife and children. In my growing years I saw many similar sacrifices that he made without complaining. I benefited from his sacrifice to send me to church school and later to The Ohio State University. I benefited from the gift of an acre of land on which to build my first home in Germantown. I benefited from the sacrifice he made for the down payment on my first home away from home in Bridgeville, Pennsylvania. I benefited from the sacrifices he made to bring me to that great day we enjoyed together—the day of my ordination into the gospel ministry.

By the time I came along, Daddy had automobiles. He had many of them over the years. He no longer walked the many miles to work. He had more than a nickel in his pockets on any given day. But I've got to tell you: I caught him cutting out cardboard, sitting by our fireplace at night. He was cutting out cardboard to put in old, worn-out shoes—even with a closet full of brand-new Romeo shoes that he loved so much. These were shoes that we, his children, had bought for him. It's truly difficult to break some habits.

When I looked at him, I understood more fully the ultimate sacrifice of Jesus for us. Daddy never had to die for us, but I believe he would have. Jesus did give His life, and I am eternally grateful for this sacrificial act that secured my salvation.

"For then must He often have suffered since the foundation of the world: but now once in the end of the world hath He appeared to put away sin by the sacrifice of Himself" (Heb. 9:26). With Jesus absolutely nothing is too good for His children. Thank You, Lord!

Twenty-five

"NOW THAT'S REAL MUSIC!"

Daddy loved music. He didn't perform music, but he loved it—vocal, instrumental, all music. He didn't have a good singing voice, but he had a definite pitch. I can remember the old days when I was a kid. Daddy would lead the church singing band out into the streets on Saturday nights after sundown to raise money for Harvest Ingathering. This was a means of collecting funds to support the church's outreach ministry in neighborhoods across America and around the world.

He always pitched the songs for the "band" to sing. "There is Joy in That Land," or "Down at the Cross," or "The Old

Rugged Cross." These old favorites and many more would waft out across the night air in autumn, and you could see the porch lights go on as our solicitors knocked on doors to allow folks to contribute to health, education, and welfare for the less fortunate.

He also loved to hear his children sing together as the Wright Family Ensemble Singers. He would slide out to the edge of his chair by the fireplace with a twinkle in his eye as we rehearsed some favorite or worked out the close harmony that was our trademark. His favorite hymn was "Higher Ground"; the favorite spiritual was "Swing Low"; and the very best gospel song was "Precious Lord." On these occasions he was never conscious for long. It seemed that our music was the perfect sleeping pill for an exhausted man at peace with God and the world.

Daddy also had a favorite popular song, and whenever it came on the radio, performed on a saxophone, his favorite instrument, he would exclaim, "Now that's real music." The song was "Sentimental Journey." A close second favorite would be "Lucky Old Sun," which he never failed to call "Lucky Old Boy."

He made a tremendous sacrifice to buy a saxophone for me, hoping one day to hear me play "Sentimental Journey." I never mastered that one, but he seemed to delight in watching me in the high school marching band and smile with pride as I performed in the high school orchestra.

Daddy believed that music was the perfect setting for rest, meditation, church, happy times, and preaching. Momma was a great singer, and all her brothers played stringed instruments that they made themselves. So Daddy surrounded himself as often as possible with the very best music he could find. You always knew he was pleased with your musical offering if you heard his familiar "Now that's real music!"

Did you know that our Heavenly Father loves good music? He has a fantastic choir in heaven made up of angels. I believe their music is unparalleled by anything we have ever heard on earth. Do you suppose that He leans forward on His throne as they render some majestic hymn of praise to Him?

I find it almost incomprehensible that the angels will fold their wings and listen when the redeemed of the earth will sing the Song of Moses and the Lamb. I want to be in that choir as they strike up this song of redemption found in Revelation 15:2-4:

"And I saw as it were a sea of glass mingled with fire: and them that had gotten the victory over the beast, and over his image, and over his mark, and over the number of his name, stand on the sea of glass, having the harps of God. And they sing the song of Moses the servant of God, and the song of the Lamb, saying,

'Great and marvelous are thy works,
Lord God Almighty;

just and true are thy ways, thou King of Saints.

Who shall fear thee, O Lord, and glorify thy name?

For thou only art holy: for all nations shall come and

worship before thee; for thy judgments are made manifest.'"

I can just hear the Father proclaim: "Now that's real music!" Please, let's not miss the great rehearsal day in glory!

Twenty-six

"BOY, I'LL GO THROUGH YOU LIKE A DOSE OF SALTS!"

Daddy used this old saying at moments when he was most frustrated with me. I must have been 16 years old before I realized that he was threatening to discipline me as thoroughly as a dose of laxative does its work. When I was much younger, I had no idea what he was talking about, but it sounded really ominous. As I mentioned elsewhere in this book, Momma was in charge of corporal punishment, but Daddy was in charge of threatening. The problem was, I didn't know when his threats would take on reality.

That brings me to the problem of the "salts." Daddy loved a roaring fire on the hearth in winter, so he needed lots of fuel. It was my job to stack logs and coal next to the fireplace. It was difficult and unpleasant work, but it was one of my chores, and Daddy expected it to be completed when he arrived home in the evening.

Most of the time I tended to this readily, but at other times I dallied and delayed until he came home. It made him very unhappy, and with good reason. Not only had I neglected to do the task we had agreed upon, but also, he was exhausted from long hours at work. He wasn't too tired to stoke the fire, however. In fact, he preferred to be the one tending the blaze, and he just needed a faithful son to conveniently place the fuel.

I don't know why I did it. It was so unlike me to challenge or respond to Daddy without his asking for a reply. He was huffing and puffing around the house as I hurried to bring in the firewood and coal. Then I said, "Daddy, even when I get the chores done early, you still come in and work just as if I haven't done anything, and that's not fair!"

What was I thinking? I had not just flown in from Mars or some other remote place in the galaxy. I knew very well that Daddy didn't accept any "back talk" from his children.

He swung around and faced me with a pretty threatening look. "Boy, don't talk back to me! Don't you know I'll go through you like a dose of salts?" Now I came up with an unsolicited response: "I'm sorry, Daddy. I didn't mean to talk back." Immediately, the color in his face returned to normal as he said, "Well, see to it that you don't!"

Man, that was a close call! It seems that we could discuss issues, but they had to be on his terms and in his time. I was no match for him, either in stature or in experience, and I was in no position to challenge him. Later, after supper, Daddy told me that he and Momma were trying to work out an allowance for me. An allowance! This man provided me with food, shelter, clothing, love, and the discipline of love. He owed me nothing more, yet he wanted to give me some spending money out of his meager wages.

Did you know that our Father God does some huffing and puffing, too, when we disobey Him? Listen: "For behold the day cometh, that shall burn as an oven; and all the proud, yea, and all that do wickedly, shall be stubble: and the day that cometh shall burn them up, saith the Lord of hosts, that it shall leave them neither root nor branch" (Mal. 4:1).

But the moment we repent and submit, He responds with, "Come now, and let us reason together, saith the Lord: though your sins be as scarlet, they shall be as white as snow; though they be like crimson, they shall be as wool" (Isa. 1:18). God doesn't really want to destroy anyone. The entire plan of salvation shows us plainly that His intention is to rescue and save every person who is willing to accept Him as Lord and Savior. His huffing and puffing is not a bluff, any more than was Daddy's. But in both cases, a loving father is giving fair warning to wayward children. We should be careful not to force either father into doing what he loathes to do. Surrender is the answer.

Twenty-seven

"Get It Done Before Sundown"

Daddy was an orthodox Seventh-day Adventist. As such, he taught and modeled strict observance of the Sabbath, which began at sundown on Friday and continued through sundown each Saturday. These sacred hours were set aside for worship, praise, and fellowship. And of course, no manual labor was performed except what was absolutely necessary. I milked the cows and fed the chickens, but that was about the extent of it.

Based on the fourth of the Ten Commandments in Exodus 20:8, Adventists cherish the Sabbath as a day of rest. Friday is a day of preparation for the Sabbath, and therefore, we all believe, as Daddy did, that you had to get all your work done before sundown on Friday.

Carl Sakaitis tilled a 200-acre farm across the road from our small 20-acre plot of land. I worked for Carl and his mom, Barbara, on many occasions as a young boy. That was another source of my farming savvy. They were extremely hard workers, and we were amazed watching them in the fields. They were bundled up head-to-toe in heavy clothing on hot summer days. I asked Barbara why they put on so many clothes, while we Americans were stripping down to the bare minimum. She replied in her heavy Romanian accent: "The same clothes that keep out the cold also keep out the heat." I tried it. She was right!

Carl and I were "making hay" on one of those hot summer days. That's the best time to mow, dry, and haul hay into barns. He mowed on Thursday, tedded or turned the hay on Friday, and then got tied up with other farm chores. I left for home in mid-afternoon and thought no more about his 35 or 40 acres of hay drying in the sun. Along toward sundown, the sky darkened a bit.

Carl showed up at our door enquiring as to what my little weather station was predicting. He was a great one for consulting the farmer's almanac and my weather station when it came to planting and harvesting crops. I told him it looked like rain, for sure. Well, if you know about farming, you know that after you turn the hay once and it dries, you must get it into the barn. If it gets wet again, and you try to ted it again, the process will knock all the leaves off the stock, and you are left with just useless stems.

That's when it happened. Carl asked my daddy if we could help him get his hay in before the rain. If not, he would lose the hay crop, which was much needed cattle feed for the winter coming on. To my total surprise, Daddy called all his sons together and announced that we were going to make hay on Friday evening! We worked until well after sundown and saved the hay crop.

103

Daddy prayed the most beautiful prayers. One was before making hay, to ask our Heavenly Father to protect us from injury as we worked. The other prayer was after the work was done, to thank God, not only for His protection, but also for the strength He had supplied us to accomplish the task. He never apologized in either prayer. What he did was quote the words of Jesus when He said, "It is lawful to do well on the Sabbath days" (Matt. 12:12). Upon reaching adulthood, I researched this idea for myself.

Isn't it interesting that our parent's faith is our faith for much of our childhood years? But the time must come for each of us to build a faith and relationship to God on our own. When I searched for this idea of lawfulness to do well on the Sabbath, I found many cross-references. My favorite is found in Luke 14:5: "And answered them, saying, 'Which of you shall have an ass or an ox fallen into a pit, and will not straightway pull him out on the Sabbath day?'"

We did not go looking for work to do on Sabbath. And neither Daddy nor any of us would have ever considered taking pay for what we had done. It was a missionary endeavor. Carl went throughout the farm community telling any who would listen about what Daddy and his boys had done to save his hay crop. He said that he knew how devout we were about our faith, and therefore he hesitated to ask. But he was desperate, and we were the only farm family he had built a relationship with.

Did things change around the Wright household after this incident? Not a whit! We all knew for sure that when it came to our secular activities, you had to "get it done before sundown."

Twenty-eight

"Mother, I Think We Have Raised a Pack of Idiots!"

There are lots of advantages to being reared in a large family. Normal social development is made easier. You learn pretty early that selfishness will not get you very far. Sharing is an everyday occurrence, and there is an abundance of hand-me-down clothes available if you're not the oldest child.

There are disadvantages also. It's a long time before you get your own bed or bedroom. Waiting for the bathroom can be a literal pain. People have a tendency to compare the accomplishments of each sibling, and that's not fair. And there is an abundance of hand-me-down clothes available if you're not the oldest child.

As stated before, we were gospel singers, though our repertoire included much more than gospel songs. Our rehearsal periods were special occasions. Sometimes they were bizarre occasions. Once, we were trying to work out some intricate harmony in a song, and we were all expressing our opinions as to how it should be performed.

Now, discussions in our family could reach fever pitch, and anyone passing by our house during one of those sessions would assume that there was a knock-down, drag-out fight going on within. Not so—it just seemed that way to the uninitiated.

On this occasion I believe we were unusually rambunctious and vocal. As a matter of fact, we may have been nearing an actual knock-down, drag-out. Daddy, who normally dozed by the fire while we sang, awoke to all this turmoil and turned to Momma with the quote that was to go down in our family history: "Mother, I think we have raised a pack of idiots!"

Many years later my nephew Clifford was interviewing Daddy for a family video, and he asked Daddy about the quote. When we play the video today we can hear the old patriarch chuckle and say, "Well, there wasn't really any meaning to that." When Cliff pressed him a little more, Daddy said, "Well, they had their ups and downs!" That is as close as he would come to criticizing his large brood of children.

I really believe the "idiot" quote came from his disappointment in the way we had lashed out at each other with such unkindness. He wanted our singing harmony to translate to our living harmony. The real test of a family may be in how it handles adversity or times of disagreement. We hadn't done very well on this occasion, and I am so glad that Daddy intervened. It was the end of those ugly flare-ups, and I can truly say good riddance.

I believe that God is often disappointed in how we treat members of the Christian family and others. The real test of Christianity may be in how we treat one another during times of adversity and disagreement. We must be careful to remember that our love for our fellow man is the strongest, and maybe the only way, that others know that we are members of the body of Christ. "By this shall all men know that ye are my disciples, if ye have love one to another" (John 13:35).

Twenty-nine

"STAY ON BOARD THE SHIP!"

Once Daddy became a Christian, his focus was on salvation for him and his family. He and Momma gave countless Bible studies in order to interest others in salvation. Long before I was born, he was a Methodist, and from the beginning, I am told that he took the Word of God very seriously.

Later, as a Seventh-day Adventist, he preached the gospel and continued to give Bible studies. They were quite a team. Daddy did the teaching, and Momma did the meditating. Let me explain. As Daddy taught, I would see my mother with the Bible open on her lap. She had her head down as if reading, but she was praying for the Holy Spirit to guide Daddy. If he needed a Bible text she would have it in an instant. It was a smooth operation.

In those days my Uncle Harlan would drive Momma and Daddy to the Bible studies. He said he couldn't teach, but he could drive the car. That was his contribution to soul-winning. He always had a car, even when Daddy didn't have one. I think for sure that Uncle Harlan will be credited with bringing some souls to Jesus.

In talking with my older siblings, I realize that they all had the experience of hearing our parents conduct Bible studies in homes around the city where we lived. The theme was always: "Jesus is coming soon." Some years later, my brother, Harold, would close each of his television programs on WHIO-TV with: "Remember, Jesus is coming again—real, real soon!"

You can see that it was ingrained in us. We believe with all our hearts that the Bible is true, and we have our parents to thank for it. Daddy often used the metaphor of a ship to describe the Church. He would say, "Stay on board the ship. The ship is going through to the kingdom."

The idea was that many discouraging situations might arise, and many tests of our faith would come, but we should not allow them to distract us from our goal of reaching heaven. We would sing the Negro spiritual, "The Old Ship of Zion." It goes like this:

> *'Tis the old ship of Zion,*
> *'Tis the old ship of Zion,*
> *'Tis the old ship of Zion,*
> *Get on board, get on board.*

> *She has landed many a thousand,*
> *She has landed many a thousand,*
> *She has landed many a thousand,*
> *Get on board, get on board.*

It will take you on to glory,
It will take you on to glory,
It will take you on to glory,
Get on board, get on board.

Yes, there are many challenges in life. If there is not a solid relationship with God, or one's faith is insecure, one might be tempted to jump ship. I think of my own bout with cancer, and the possible discouragement that lay before me. The prayers of many on my behalf, and the words of my father ringing in my ears, brought the courage that I needed. I have the assurance that God has never left me. His love and mercy endures forever.

As the apostle Paul said to the centurion and soldiers, "Unless ye abide in the ship, ye cannot be saved" (Acts 27:31).

She will anchor in God's harbor,
She will anchor in God's harbor,
She will anchor in God's harbor,
Stay on board, stay on board.

"You Can Always Come Home"

When Daddy told me this, it was understood that wherever he and Momma resided was to be considered "home." It meant that no matter where we children were or whatever circumstances we found ourselves in, we could come to him. He was saying that no difficulty we encountered would make us ineligible to return to the sure comfort he was able to supply.

He did not mean that anything we did would be acceptable. He was not saying that he would uphold us in doing wrong. The message was clear that he loved us without condition, and that we would always be welcome, no matter what. That is a wonderful thing to know if you are far from home and hurting.

Daddy and Momma never encouraged us to come running to them if we had a crisis in our marriages, but we knew we could come for good, solid, Bible-based counsel. I recall a difficulty early in my own marriage. I came for comfort, and they wrote beautiful letters of encouragement to my wife. Daddy refused to take sides, and his door was open to both of us. We have now passed the half-century mark in marriage, and I can thank God for parents who were kind and just and impartial.

I began my ministry as a lay pastor in my home church in Germantown, Ohio. Upon leaving the Seventh-day Adventist Theological Seminary, my first assignment as a full-time pastor was back in Germantown. After serving there for three years, we were re-assigned to the Pittsburgh-Uniontown, Pennsylvania, district. That was a tough move, but for the first time Jackie and I had the feeling that we had established a home away from home. I could no longer walk across the lawn to Daddy's house for suggestions on agenda items for my church board meetings. There was the telephone, but it was just not the same.

I remember the frequent trips back to Germantown at first and how they gradually became less frequent. I was 40 years old but still cherished encounters with my father. A few years later we were called to serve in the Allegheny West Conference office in Columbus, Ohio, which meant we were only 80 miles from "home." The trips were rare but joyously anticipated. I even did a brief stint as interim pastor in Germantown.

One day I had a call from Dr. Burks, Daddy's personal physician. He said, "Your dad is very ill. He has been sent to the hospital, but it doesn't look good."

I am sure that Ohio's speed laws were broken as I drove to Sycamore Hospital in Miamisburg. I sat in the waiting room for over an hour after being told that someone would speak to me about Daddy. I should have known then. I was not allowed to see him. Finally, a nurse came by and asked if I had been waited on. I said that I was waiting for word on my father, Nathan Wright. She replied, "Oh, I'm so sorry, but Mr. Wright was expired on arrival."

Hot tears coursed down my cheeks as I tried to take in what she was saying. Daddy is gone? Impossible! He was the strongest person I ever knew. If he was gone, what happens to "home?" Well, he really was gone—and home would never be the same. Momma slipped rapidly into dementia, and four years later she fell asleep in Jesus.

Now it meant that I would have to establish a "home" for my children and their spouses—a place of comfort and joy. We have been able to do that, and now we know the feeling Daddy had when we arrived on his doorstep. He would bellow out, "Mother, the kids are here!" Yes, we could always come home.

I now look forward to my real home. It is a place where we will not know pain and suffering, or parting and death. "Let not your heart be troubled: ye believe in God, believe also in me. In my father's house are many mansions: if it were not so, I would have told you. I go to prepare a place for you. And if I go and prepare a place for you, I will come again, and receive you unto myself; that where I am, there ye may be also" (John 14:1-3).

Can't you hear Jesus saying, "You can always come home?"

PHOTOGRAPHIC
Memories

*Nathan Monroe Wright and Willa Dale
(Daddy and Momma) were married in 1915.*

Walter L. Wright was 12 years old in 1946.

On a Sabbath afternoon in 1958,
Momma and Daddy stopped for a picture
before leaving to give Bible studies.

Momma and Daddy lived in Germantown,
Ohio when this photo was taken in 1972.

*This picture of Walter with Daddy
and Momma was taken in 1975.*

*Daddy's "green thumb" is hidden
behind his championship zucchini squash.*

Momma and Daddy celebrated their 65th wedding anniversary in 1980.